GW01142520

Blooming Rooms

QUARRY

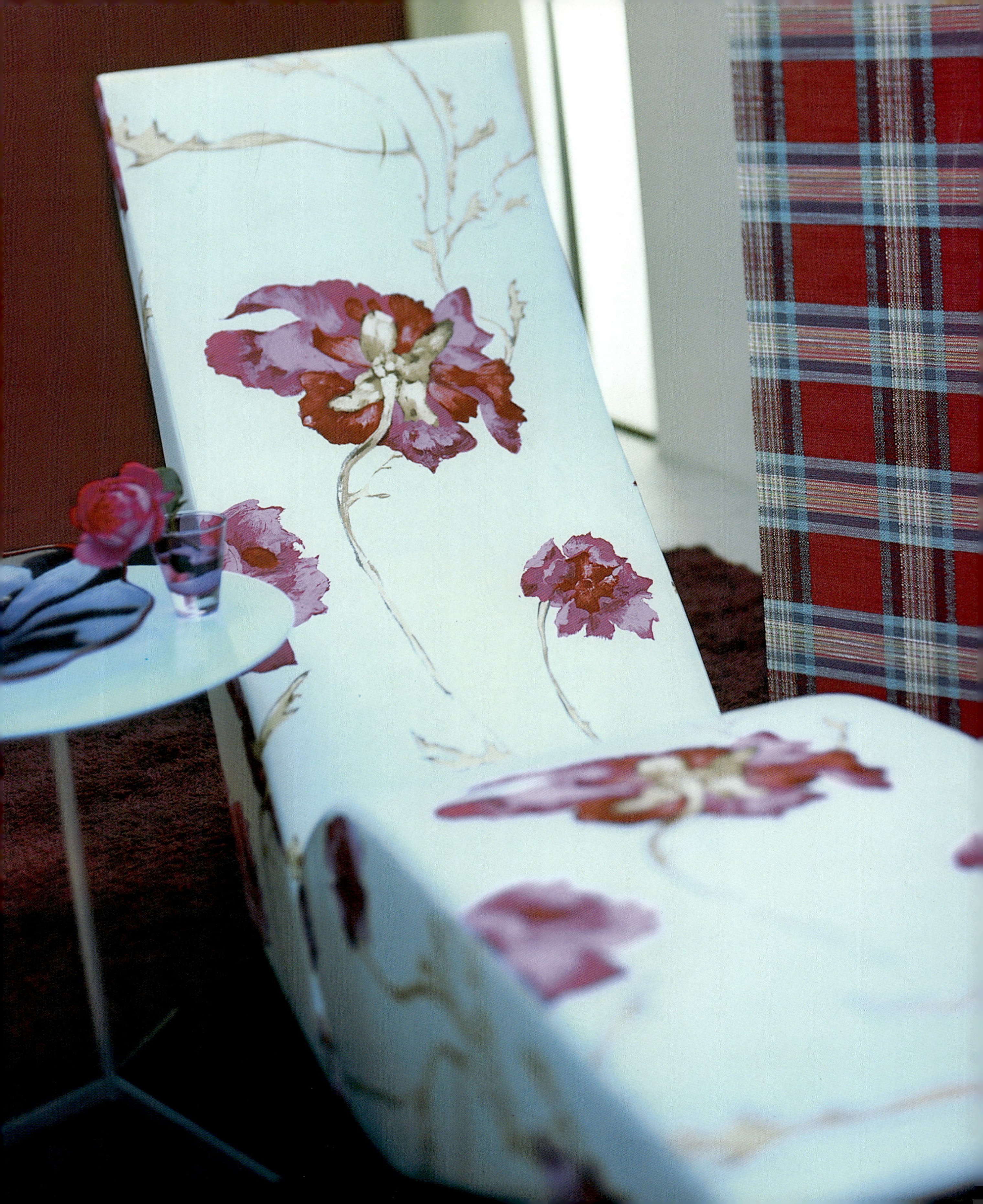

GLOUCESTER MASSACHUSETTS

Blooming Rooms
DECORATING WITH FLOWERS AND FLORAL MOTIFS

QUARRY BOOKS

A. Bronwyn Llewellyn and Meera Lester

© 2004 by Quarry Books

All rights reserved. No part of this book may be reproduced in any form without written permission of the copyright owners. All images in this book have been reproduced with the knowledge and prior consent of the artists concerned, and no responsibility is accepted by producer, publisher, or printer for any infringement of copyright or otherwise, arising from the contents of this publication. Every effort has been made to ensure that credits accurately comply with information supplied.

First published in the United States of America by
Quarry Books, and imprint of
Rockport Publishers, Inc.
33 Commercial Street
Gloucester, Massachusetts 01930-5089
Telephone: (978) 282-9590
Fax: (978) 283-2742
www.rockpub.com

Library of Congress Cataloging-in-Publication Data
Llewellyn, A. Bronwyn (Anita Bronwyn)
    Blooming rooms : decorating with flowers and floral motifs / Anita Bronwyn Llewellyn and Meera Lester.
       p.   cm.
    ISBN 1-59253-015-X (hardcover)
    1. Interior decoration—Themes, motives. 2. Decoration and ornament—Plant forms.
3. Floral decorations. I. Lester, Meera. II. Title.
NK2115.5.P49L54 2004
747'.98—dc22   2003018546
                                                                   CIP

ISBN 1-59253-015-X

10 9 8 7 6 5 4 3 2 1

Design: Yee Design
Cover and Spine Images: Courtesy of Zimmer + Rohde, www.zimmer-rohde.com
Back Cover: (left to right) Courtesy of Mariposa; (2nd from left) Courtesy of Laura Ashley, Ltd;
    (2nd from right) Courtesy of Sanderson;

Printed in China

I dedicate this book to the three women who shaped my life and instilled in me a love of flowers: my mother, Elizabeth Louise, who loved lilacs and roses; my grandmother, Rosa Lee, who adored the pink peonies growing near her farmhouse in Boone County, Missouri; and Aunt Dilla Lue, who is currently captivated by lilies.

— Meera Lester

Everything I know about flowers and gardening I learned from four people: my father, Urban Beadle Llewellyn, Meera Lester, Joan Ishiwata, and Laramie Treviño. My heartfelt thanks to all.

— A. Bronwyn Llewellyn

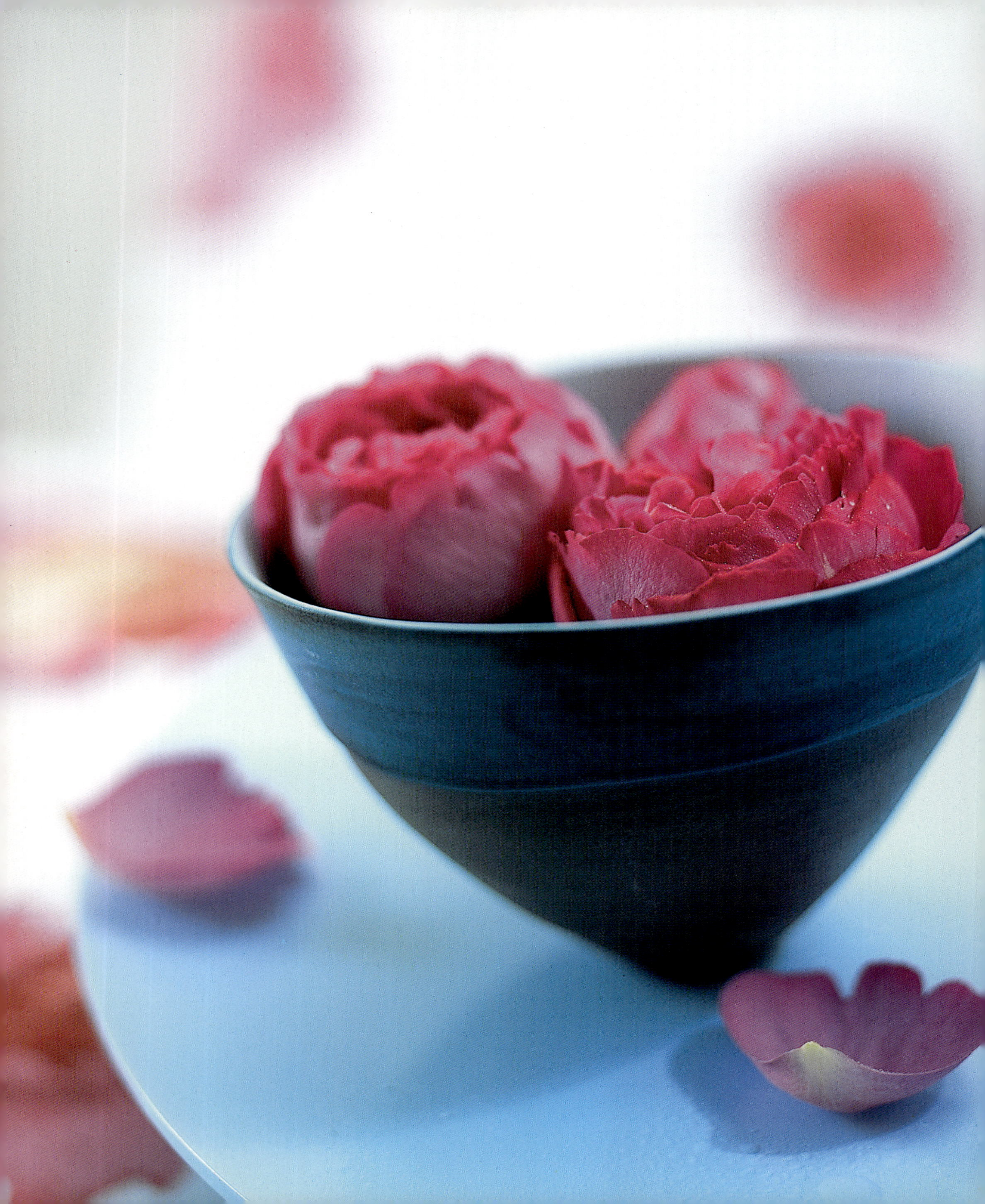

Contents

- **8**   An Introduction to the History of Flowers in the Home

- **10**   The Blooming Room Plan
  - *20*   *Flowers through History: Lotus Blossoms Embodied Rich Symbolism in Ancient Egypt*

- **22**   Blooming Entries
  - *32*   *Flowers through History: The Greeks Preferred Stylized Flowers; Romans Wanted Realism*

- **34**   Blooming Living Rooms
  - *54*   *Flowers through History: Asian Artisans Created Realistic and Symbolic Flower Embellishments*
  -       *Many Indian Floral Patterns Have Survived Unchanged*

- **56**   Blooming Kitchens
  - *64*   *Flowers through History: Byzantine and Celtic Cultures Developed Complex Floral Motifs*
  -       *Rosettes and Rich Patterns Characterized Florals of the Middle Ages*

- **66**   Blooming Dining Rooms
  - *78*   *Flowers through History: Persian Decorative Arts Bloomed with Flowers Flowers Have Always*
  -       *Been Inextricably Linked with Carpet Design*

- **80**   Blooming Bedrooms and Baths
  - *92*   *Flowers through History: European Ornamentation Flowered in Renaissance, Baroque,*
  -       *and Rococo Styles*

- **94**   Blooming Indoor Garden Rooms
  - *110*   *Flowers through History: Mechanization and Eclectic Tastes Filled Homes with Anything Floral*

- **112**   Blooming Accents and Accessories
  - *122*   *Flowers through History: Motifs of the Past Inspired Arts and Crafts Floral Arrangements*

- **124**   Blooming Outdoor Garden Rooms
  - *132*   *Flowers through History: Art Nouveau Embraced Fantastical Flower and Tendril Motifs*
  -       *Simple Folk Motifs Continued the Floral Tradition*
  -       *Contemporary Florals Look to the Past—and the Future*

- **136**   Bibliography

- **138**   Resources

- **141**   Photography Credits

- **142**   About the Authors

- **144**   Acknowledgments

An Introduction to the History of Flowers in the Home

Blooming Rooms & the Art of the Flower

Like these favorites of Nature, every ornament should have its perfume, i.e., the reason for its application.

— Owen Jones

Was there ever a time when flowers didn't adorn living spaces? Imagine an early cave-dweller returning from some foray clutching a fistful of weedy flowers wrenched from the dirt—a few cheerful blossoms to give off a faint scent more pleasing than that of animal fat or charred logs. Without a doubt, ever since humankind learned to smear pigments into recognizable patterns, weave fibers into textiles, and carve stone and wood into useful objects, decorative inspiration has come from the natural world. And what could be easier than symmetrically repeating a simple shape, like an oval, to make a flower?

Owen Jones, in his *Grammar of Ornament*, first published in 1856, juxtaposes every sort of style, including floral, across cultures and through time. His color plates make it easy to see patterns and similarities among flower motifs as they traveled around the globe to be reinterpreted over and over again. Many millennia-old palmettes, rosettes, and other decorations remain startlingly current. If you can't find certain motifs now, don't worry. Someday they'll be in vogue again, because in the design world, nothing really goes away. The history of flowers in decoration is one of perpetual cycles of trends, not unlike the perennials in your garden that come to life and die out season after season. Whether you lean toward modern, country, romantic, exotic, or classical motifs, today you have every style from every historical period at your fingertips.

In addition to the decorating ideas presented here for each room of the home, at the end of each chapter you will find sidebars on floral motifs and objects that characterize various periods throughout history. If you see styles that interest you, search for additional decorating inspiration on the Internet. Look through old books and periodicals. Visit museums, botanical gardens, and historic houses. Study posters, portraits, paintings, and other illustrations for clues to the home embellishments of their period.

You'll also find creative sidebars on everything from making homemade scented pastilles to decorating lampshades to painting flowers on furniture and floors. Everywhere you look there are floral ideas that you can interpret for your home in fresh, new ways. Pick the best among all that you find to make your own distinctive "blooming" rooms.

above *Watch the room spring to life when you mix a yellow poppy pattern on orchid wallpaper with linens of chartreuse, red-violet, and the poppy hue in bright stripes.*

The Blooming Room Plan

I know a little garden close,
Set thick with lily and red rose,
Where I might wander if I might
From dewy morn to dewy night

— William Morris

The legendary William Morris didn't need a road map to get to his garden. And, judging from his legacy of pattern, color, design, and furniture, he didn't need any help planning and executing an artistic blooming room. But some of us do. A master plan helps minimize expensive mistakes and makes it more likely that you will achieve the look that inspired you in the first place. Before you start pulling together a particular look for a blooming room, consider the following:

Size or scale — Select patterns and colors carefully so as not to overpower a tiny space or make a large space look too sterile and empty. For example, large-print wallpaper that looks great in a large space will seem to shrink an already small room.

Purpose of the room — Consider lively colors and durable and washable fabrics in family rooms, dining rooms, and kitchens where food and beverages are served. Choose restful colors and comfortable or luxurious fabrics for bedrooms and baths.

Traffic patterns — Give special consideration to floor and furniture coverings in entries and kitchens, since they usually bear the most traffic.

Dramatic elements — Factor these into an overall room plan or build your new room around them.

Problem areas — Study any unusual angular configurations (window shapes, ceiling slopes, built-in shelves in an odd location, etc.). Decide whether you will dramatize or minimize them.

Search for Textures, Patterns, and Color Palettes That Inspire You

Visit fabric stores. Most feature a section with fabrics for the home. There are also stores that cater solely to the home decorator. Study in-store displays to see how professionals create a look by mixing and coordinating fabric patterns, textures, and colors. Also notice how they use reversals of pattern and color as well as scale to accomplish their aims. Read through the following list of fabrics that are often used in the home and consider how you might incorporate them into your dream room.

Acrylic ~ fabric made of strong, synthetic fibers that won't shrink

Brocade ~ a heavy silk fabric that is sumptuous in appearance, often with gold and silver threads woven throughout

Burlap ~ coarsely woven cloth made from jute, hemp, or flax

Calico ~ smooth, brightly printed cloth, usually cotton

Cambric ~ a finely woven white linen or cotton fabric

Challis ~ a lightweight and versatile fabric made of wool, rayon, or cotton

Chambray ~ a fine, lightweight fabric woven with white threads over a colored warp to produce solids, stripes, and checks

Chenille ~ soft fabric made of tufted cotton or silk

Chintz ~ a large-print, floral, glazed fabric often used in curtains

Damask ~ a richly patterned, reversible, jacquard weave of silk, wool, cotton, or synthetic fibers

Dotted Swiss ~ sheer fabric with dots woven throughout, often used for curtains

Flannel ~ woven cloth of wool or a blend of cotton, synthetics, and wool in which one or both sides have a napped surface

Gingham ~ cotton that has a checkered pattern and is often used for curtains and pillow covers

India print ~ brightly colored, hand-blocked prints on cotton

Linen ~ lustrous, smooth, strong cloth woven from the fibers of flax

left *Heads will turn when spectacular blooms like these are contrasted against a plain upholstered chair and throw.*

Matelassé ~ woven fabric with a quilt-like surface often used for bed coverlets and pillow shams

Lace ~ a delicate, weblike fabric of thread or yarn, used for curtains, tablecloths, and as decorative edging

Paisley ~ soft wool or some other natural fabric with a multicolored, woven or printed pattern of swirls or abstract, curvilinear shapes derived from the ancient Persian teardrop motif

Silk ~ soft, lustrous, natural fiber produced by silkworms

Toile du Jouy ~ a sheer cotton or linen fabric depicting pictorial scenes against a white or ivory background

Twill ~ durable cotton fabric with diagonal parallel ribs

Wool ~ a natural textile made from the hair or fur of sheep and other mammals

With certain fabrics, weave and texture dictate how your eye perceives the color. Also, color looks different depending on whether you see it in natural light, under fluorescent lamps, or by candlelight. Some fabrics glitter, sparkle, and reflect light; some dazzle with iridescence; and others quietly absorb and tone down color, especially intense color. Still others, with flower shapes worked in embroidery or created with lace, mirror art, sequins, or beading, boldly satisfy the need for pattern, texture, and color in one fell swoop. Finally, fabric with tone-on-tone flowers woven into it provides a floral motif but gives the appearance of a solid color.

Consider fabric swatches in colors that ordinarily you might not choose. For example, red-violet and its opposite on the color wheel, yellow-green (or chartreuse), are absolutely stunning together. So are couplings of the same colors in a softer intensity—plum and sage. Don't limit yourself. And remember, one or two colors are nice, but three or more greatly increase your options. Note how many colors are in each swatch. What is the dominant color? What is the pattern? Is the texture right? Will the color and pattern contribute to the overall feel of the room you want to create? Choose those with interrelated colors or mix them for an unusual and exotic look.

below Chartreuse and green apple paired with red-violet, plum, and orchid bloom dramatically in decorator fabrics.

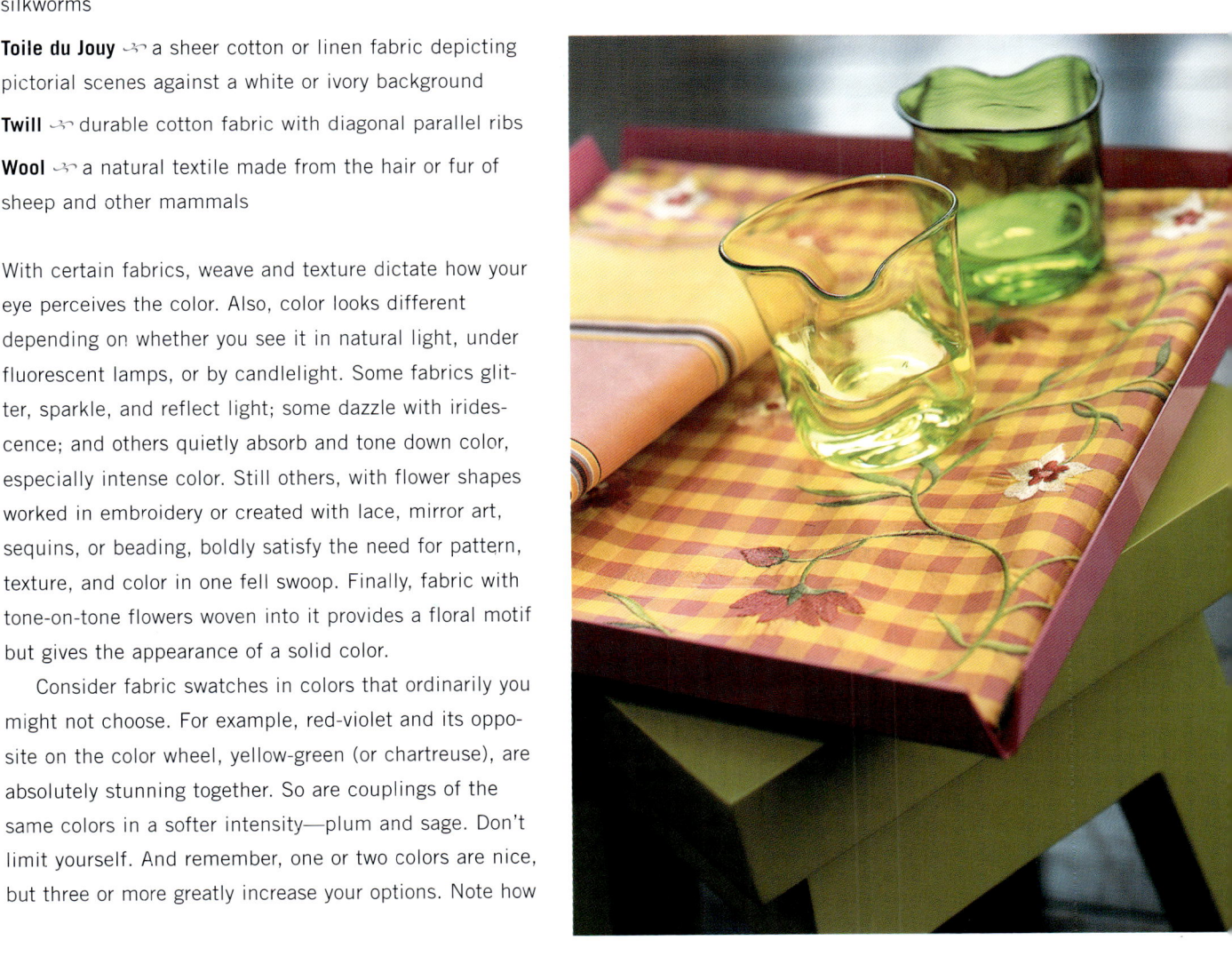

You have lots of pattern choices, including checks, florals, stripes, plaids, animal prints, paisleys, abstract designs, pictorial images, and polka dots. Request swatches of the fabrics you like. Take them home. Go into the rooms where those fabrics will live, lay them out on a flat surface or table, and play around with combinations. Put paint and wallpaper samples with the fabric swatches to see what works and what doesn't in terms of pattern, color, and scale. But don't throw away any swatch just because it doesn't look right with the others. There are techniques to unify disparate patterns. Also, don't forget that such elements as hardwood floors or a quarried, colored stone fireplace will contribute their color and texture to a room. Furniture, too, provides texture, pattern, and color. See for yourself. Move in a stunning piece of furniture that has been painted a lively color and features some artistic element like a carved or painted flower motif and notice what it contributes to the space.

Patterns on walls can be created several ways: hand-painted, stenciled, textured (using a variety of methods), or wallpapered. Wallpaper patterns, however, can be a little tricky. Just remember to think of scale above all else. Vertical stripes draw the eye upward, making the walls seem taller. Horizontal stripes widen or expand the space. Unify striped wallpaper (that goes from floor to chair-rail height) and the floral patterned paper used above it by adding a color- and pattern-coordinated border at the seam where the two patterns meet. Keep the wallpaper pattern simple for a living room to avoid having it compete with other elements.

Now you have the basic idea of how to develop a master plan. Use the following guidelines as departure points from which you can begin your own journey into blooming room style.

14 *Blooming Rooms*

Mix, Match, Coordinate, and Integrate for Eight Different Looks

Jungle or Tropical

Use a patterned fabric of flowers, ferns, or palms in the colors of earth and forest (or camouflage colors) for upholstery, pillows, and curtains. Coordinate that fabric with wallpaper. Pick a solid color from the fabric and wallpaper to make linings for drapes, to cover accent or floor pillows, or to create a canopy over a daybed or couch. Add animal-patterned accent pillows in the same color scheme. Finish the look by putting out an old suitcase, a few travel books and maps, floral-scented pillar candles, jungle flower prints, and plants and palms in baskets. For a kid's room, hang a fishnet canopy in a corner, anchoring the net three-fourths of the way up the two walls. Load the canopy with stuffed animals, including monkeys scurrying up the ropes.

Country

Select colorful calico prints, vintage quilts, or wildflower motifs associated with American, European, or Scandinavian rural style. Find country-style furniture (antiques or reproductions, if you're going for an authentic look; painted furniture, if you're not). Use three to four main colors to unify everything. Coordinate quilt patterns, paint, or wallpaper as well as the trim on slipcovers, bed skirts, and pillows. Keep the colors light and airy for a Swedish look, bolder and brighter for a European look, and warm and sunny for an American country look. Abundantly use country accents and lots of flowers.

Classic

Blend flower patterns of blue and white and gray. Or, to create a timeless appeal, coordinate ivory or yellow with navy and burgundy. Also consider shades of brown, black, or white with red accents. Use formal-style piping and pleats, for example, on upholstered, patterned couches and chairs. Add drapery tiebacks of thick, colored cords and tassels. Colored stripes (like drapery trim or striped wallpaper) look lovely against floral patterns used elsewhere in the room in the same colors. Furniture, artwork, lamps, and rugs with crisp, clean lines will look best.

Natural

Use linens, cottons, silk, and wool in neutral colors, or jazz up the interior with vibrant colors and exquisite floral patterns. Let accents echo those found in the natural environment—wood, metal, water, earth, air, and fire. For a warmer feeling, hang a botanical wall-print or wallpaper with floral patterns and colors of the countryside—hollyhock red, buttercup yellow, cornflower blue, grass green, primrose purple, and butterfly flower orange. Make colorful chair or

above Red rules—and unifies—in this room where two scales are working in tandem in both the floral and plaid patterns.

opposite Notice how the patterns and color combine for a light and airy feeling.

pillow cushions and curtains in these patterns, reversing them in rugs and accents. Add furniture in warm tones.

Contemporary

Establish an ebony, white, and dove gray color scheme for walls, floors, and trim. Add blistering red. Since red energizes, use it judiciously in bedrooms. For example, cover a bed with sheets of solid white patterned with eraser-size black polka dots or small, round flowers. Choose white for the bed skirt and duvet. Trim them in black piping. Or make them black. Trim with white piping. Make shams to match. Toss on an armful of accent pillows in various shapes and sizes: a red-patterned silk pillow with black tassels; an elaborate, floral-patterned gray silk with black trim; a white silk with a black flower; and a black silk featuring a white flower such as a gardenia or white hyacinth.

Old-World Elegance

Use floral brocades, damasks, solid velvets, moirés, chintz, or silky, striped fabrics in cool greens, blues, and ivory for drapes, pillows, and upholstered furniture. Don't skimp on fabric. Hang heavy drapes festooned with a swag that has been lavishly embroidered in an ancient or medieval floral pattern. Repeat the pattern in needlepoint pillows and table linens. Install tiebacks with an ancient palmette motif. For a warmer feel, paint walls a Tuscan orange (a mix of yellow ochre, raw umber, and a dash of cadmium red). Decorate with paisley fabrics in regal red, reddish-orange, gold, and burnished bronze. Be generous with floral trims, gold threadwork, and silk tassels. Over a doorway, hang a richly patterned paisley or floral portiere. Pull it to one side into an ornate, burnished gold tieback. Add an arrangement of silk flowers in the colors of gold, reddish-orange, and green. Put down a luxurious carpet repeating the flower patterns in the room. Hang a tapestry.

Victoriana Romantic

Choose lush fabrics such as silks, brocades, and sheers in monochromatic shades of champagne, gold, pinkish-brown, and rose-brown with flower and vine patterns. Use ribbon or silk roses, the symbolic flower of romantic love, to cover or trim accent pillows and silk lampshades. Embellish other pillows with bugle beads and seed pearls sewn into a rose motif. Infuse a bedroom with romance by throwing a champagne-colored duvet over the bed. Match it with a four-poster silk canopy edged in gold or rose-brown buds. Craft a dozen or more quarter-size ribbon roses and randomly sew them onto a panel of fine netting to make a throw. Edge it with a band of ivory satin and silk fringe. Fold the throw and lay it across the foot of the bed. Put a vase of fresh pink roses on the dresser and bedside table. Find pillar candles in different heights with rose petals embedded and group three or more on or next to a mirror for added reflection.

opposite *Bright yellow poppies energize an otherwise neutral color scheme of gray, chocolate, black, and white in this contemporary interior. The throw rug's loose texture offers contrast to the numerous smooth surfaces in the room.*

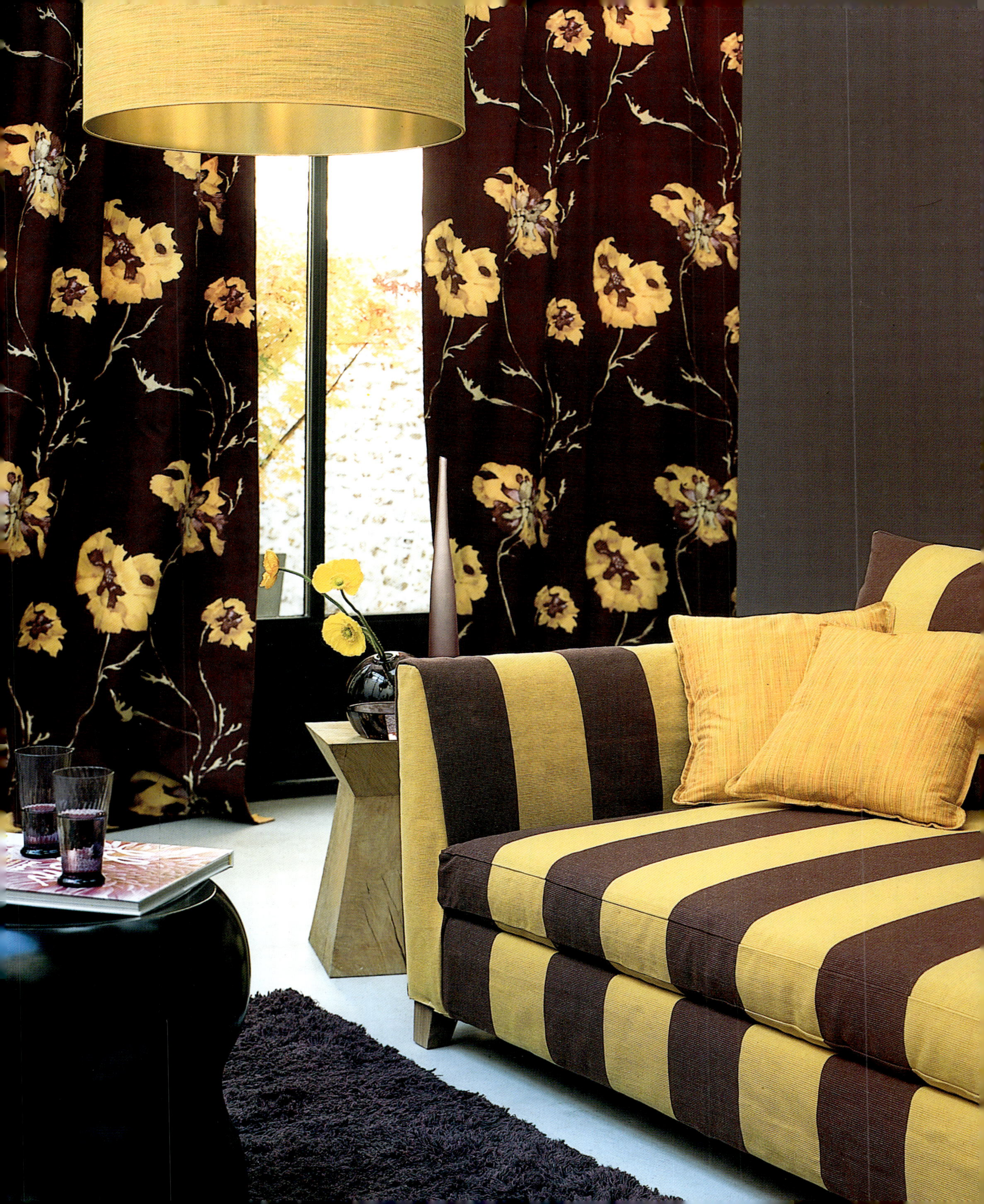

Mix and Match
THE ART OF USING FLORAL PATTERNS WITH GEOMETRICS, STRIPES, AND SOLIDS

Use these four simple methods to mix and match seemingly disparate patterns.

- **Unify through color**—Make sure the fabric patterns each have the same color scheme, that is, they feature the same basic colors in a similar tone and intensity of hue.
- **Unify through texture**—Repeat a texture, such as the ribbing of corduroy or the smooth surface of silk, in upholstered furniture, curtains, lampshades, etc., throughout a room.
- **Unify through scale**—Keep patterns of flowers, geometrics, and stripes roughly the same scale so the design elements can work harmoniously together.
- **Unify through reversals**—Try reversing both pattern and color to provide visual interest.

right *Flowers of the same colors and size in the curtains and pillows effectively allow all the other elements in the room to work together harmoniously to define the space.*

Decorate Ceramics
FROM PAINT TO PIQUE ASSIETTE MOSAIC

The Italians are masters at making beautiful floral patterns on dishware and pottery. With a little practice, you can do it, too. Paint directly onto ceramics, or use special glazing paints to draw your flowers on greenware intended to be fired in a kiln. Use these simple Italian brush strokes with three types of brushes.

- **Angle brush**—Twirl to make a half moon or new moon. Half moons made consecutively around the mouth or base of a bowl create the border. Two half moons (facing one another) form the center of a rose or a basic flower.

- **Round brush**—Make a long, swooping motion top and bottom. Lines meet at the corners. Fill the center. Voila! You've made a leaf. Use a lighter shade for highlights and a darker shade for shadow. Also, the round brush dabbed once against the greenware makes a perfect pansy petal. Repeat for multiple petals.

- **Liner brush**—Loosely outline everything you've painted on the greenware. When fired, the piece blossoms in color.

right *An ordinary terra-cotta pot "blooms" with ceramic flowers, leaves, flat-sided marbles, china shards, and shells.*

Don't like painting? Try pique assiette mosaics. This folk art form uses broken china, colored glass, bits of pottery, and found objects like old jewelry, perfume bottle stoppers, ceramic figurines, coins, buttons, keys, etc., to make new works of art.

Here are some ways to use pique assiette mosaic:

- Create a stunning frame around your fireplace or the outside edge of a mantel.
- Make a new top for an accent table.
- Create a beautiful metal container to hold fireplace andirons.
- Dramatize ordinary lamp bases.
- Adorn a wooden hostess tray.
- Beautify a frame for a mirror or clock.
- Craft an exquisite columnar base for a glass coffee table.

Flowers through History

Lotus Blossoms Embodied Rich Symbolism in Ancient Egypt

The ancient Egyptians revered the lotus as the first flower of spring and a symbol of the earth's beneficence. Artisans covered sarcophagi, bas-reliefs, water vessels, and other objects with repeated patterns of the stylized blossoms, and the motif persisted unchanged for thousands of years. The lotus appeared on ritual and everyday objects, as well as architectural elements like walls and the capitals of columns. The extremely popular rosette—a round, stylized flower as seen from above—remained a major floral motif into the Middle Ages and beyond.

The Egyptians used flowers in other ways, too. Carved furniture and painted linen sometimes featured bouquets and undulating floral friezes. Lavish baskets of fruits and flowers decorated banquet tables. And Cleopatra covered her palace floors with several inches of rose petals, an extravagance with a fragrance fit for an empress.

Egyptian floral patterns used in Western Asia, Greece, and throughout the Mediterranean contributed to the ubiquitous fan-shaped palmette common in Greece and elsewhere into modern times. Around 1800, Napoleon's Egypt campaign popularized these exotic designs in Paris and the rest of Europe, just as the discovery of King Tutankhamen's tomb did again in the 1920s. Throughout history, textiles helped to disseminate floral and other patterns from culture to culture, and in this way Egyptian floral motifs showed up in Cyprus, Syria, Palestine, and Siberia. Their traces can be seen on painted pottery and walls in Crete, where Minoan artists depicted tulips, roses, sunflowers, and irises.

opposite *Nearly 4,000 years ago, Minoan artisans on the island of Crete decorated their pottery with bold floral designs like this sunflower rosette.*

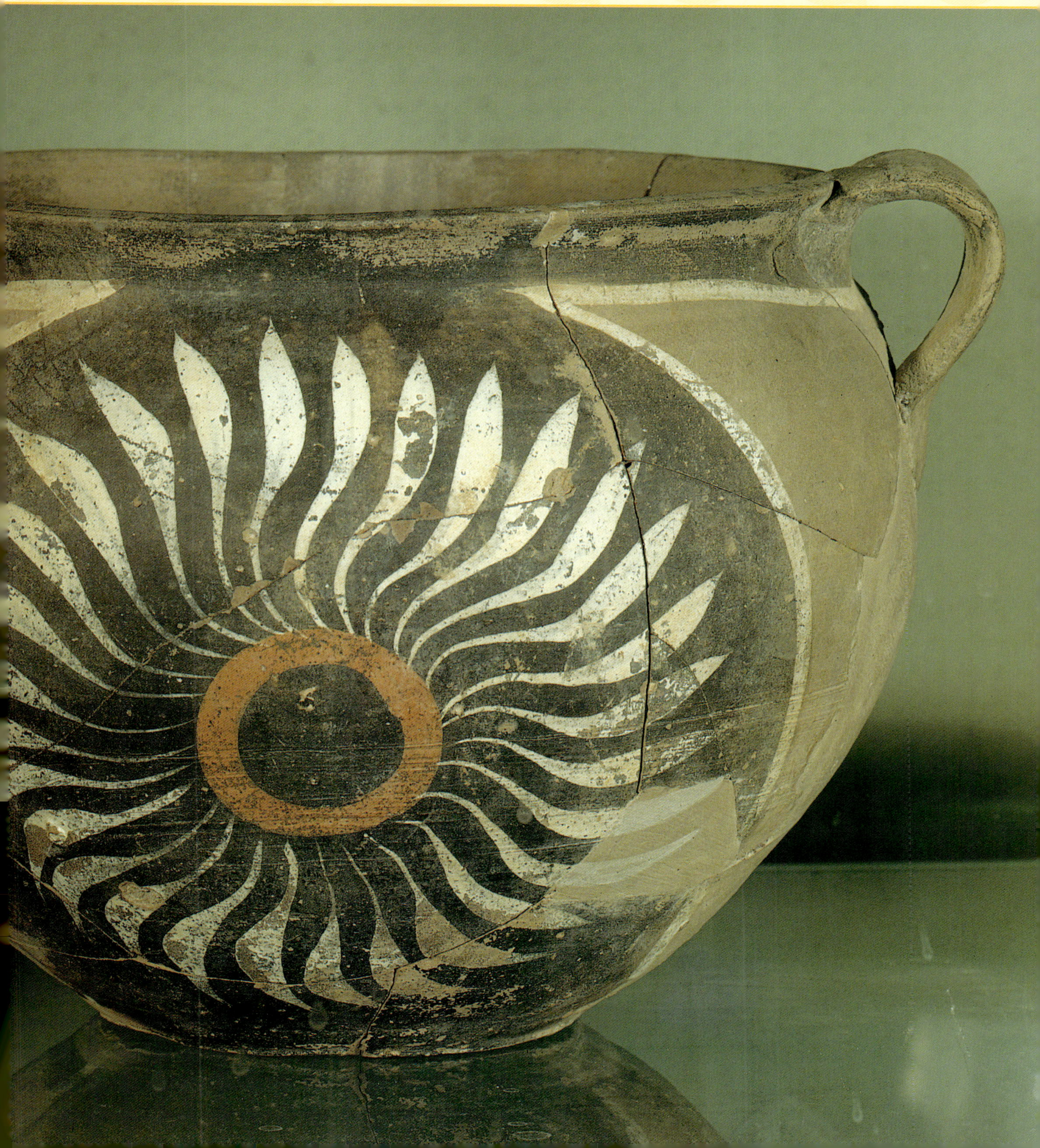

Blooming Entries

We always feel welcome when, on entering a room, we find a display of flowers on the table. Where there are flowers about, the hostess appears glad, the children pleased, the very dog and cat grateful for our arrival.

— Shirley Hibberd

Entryways were born for flowers, especially those big, splashy sprays that are too ostentatious for any other room in the house. They're a terrific way to welcome guests into your home, and they'll gladden your heart every time you come through the door. But daily fresh flowers aren't the only way to make your entry bloom.

The entry is the one room you pass through every day, probably many times a day. It can be a colorless catchall for umbrellas and keys or a cheerful salutation that sets the tone for the rest of the home. As a bridge between outdoors and inside it can encompass elements of each. Practicality requires that it withstand water, even mud, and possibly provide space for coats and parcels. Decoratively, however, the entry offers more latitude than a living room or bedroom.

The entry is undoubtedly smaller than other rooms and is used often but briefly. Its look should meld with that of adjoining rooms, but it doesn't need to match them exactly. For these reasons it can be a bit flamboyant—even over the top, if you like. A dazzling piece of furniture, a bold color, or an unusual wall covering can be perfect here. Just remember that the entry is still a functional space, and too much clutter or too little light can be hazardous.

opposite *Blooms strewn on floors, walls, and furniture warmly welcome guests in this beautiful yet functional entry.*

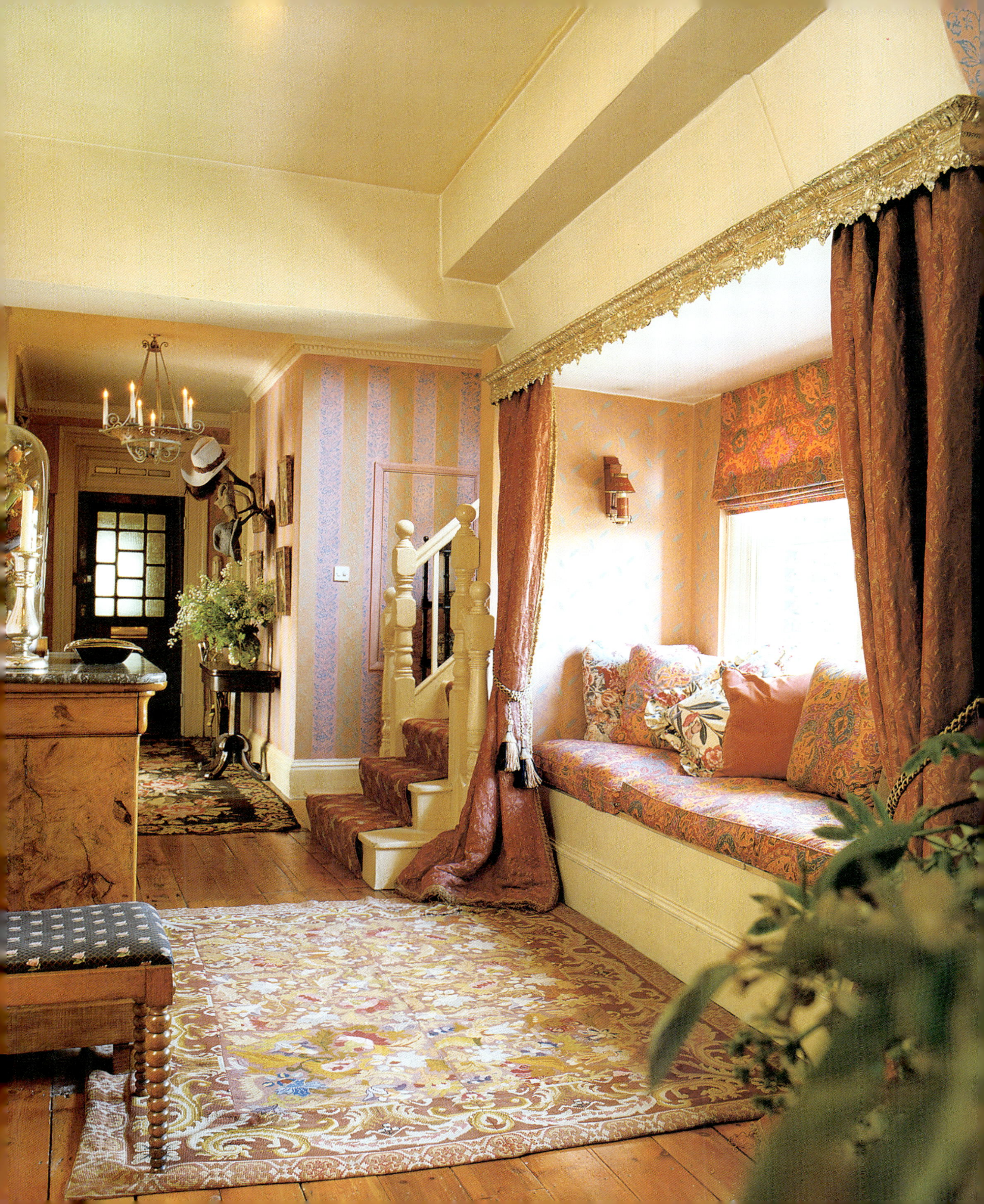

Use Flowers to Vary the Entry with the Seasons

There's a saying, "You never get a second chance to make a first impression." That may be true for people, but it doesn't have to apply to your entry. With floral details and fresh or faux flowers you can alter the mood, look, and style of the space every month of the year. Nothing could be easier than adding lavish flowers in a stunning container. Purple, coral, or golden China asters will add fire to any décor. Fresh flowers don't have to be an out-of-reach extravagance. Plant a few containers or a small plot with a cutting garden and enjoy the blooms in vases or wall pockets in the entry. Confine an abundant flowering plant in an ornate Victorian birdcage. No room for a big vase? Put up a wallpaper tromp l'oeil stone niche complete with its own bouquet. It won't take up an inch but will add lots of pizzazz.

Borrow an idea the Japanese have practiced for centuries and bring out only those items that are appropriate to the occasion and the season. That way each object gets to shine without competing for attention. Layer bamboo shelving with small floral prints or paintings and rotate the private display as you please. If the entry has a closet, replace the door with a panel of gorgeous floral fabric: tapestry or brocade in winter, a light cotton print for summer. Create seasonal arrangements of realistic silk flowers for long-lasting decorations that can be changed every few months. Bring some of the spring garden inside with large terra-cotta pots, a wrought-iron bench with pretty floral cushions, and a weathered length of garden trellis to use as a coat and hat rack.

Pretend You're Filling an Indoor Container Garden

Just as a container garden needs an "anchor" plant, and a living room a focal point, give your entryway a floral center. The accents and details will sprout from there. With a large central piece in a small entry, you won't need much more—rug, umbrella stand, coat rack, perhaps. An anchor should be in scale with the entry's size and introduce the tone, style, and mood of the home, but beyond that you can let your imagination blossom.

Bare walls don't beckon guests in. If you're artistically minded, paint free-form flower patterns or decoupage a realistic garden on the wall. One floor-to-ceiling mirrored panel makes the area seem larger and immediately doubles any floral details in the space. Perhaps you love an extravagantly expensive floral wallpaper, but your budget precludes using it in a whole room. Cover one entry wall or use a hanging panel instead. Or try grouping framed squares of several related floral papers. Digital technologies open even more design possibilities. Paper one wall with a large-scale floral photomural. Increased to giant size, the petal striations and other intricate details turn into colorful abstractions. The size and impact of colossal blooms can divert attention away from any architectural defects or anomalies in the space. As an alternative, smaller, digitally manipulated flowers create their own repetitive print.

above One way to make a small entry appear larger—and perhaps add the view you wish you had—is to paint a garden scene on one wall. There are also many wallpaper choices, from windows opening onto fanciful flowerbeds to niches of bouquet-filled vases, that "fool the eye" and add interest and depth to an entryway.

opposite A simple bamboo console paired with real and painted flowers and a treasured collection offer an entry focal point that's easily changed.

An entry can stand up to a big piece of furniture, such as a painted chest or chair, or a console inlaid with flower motifs. Assemble a large focal point out of several smaller elements, such as a table, lamp, mirror, and pot of flowers. Smooth floral fabric over a flea-market, parsons-style console and seal with polyurethane for a unique and useful piece of furniture.

Don't forget to look down. Practicality suggests a floor that's impervious to water, but that doesn't preclude flowers. Vinyl flooring, ceramic tiles, and area rugs embellished with floral motifs are plentiful and varied. Herringbone brick can mimic a garden path and meld perfectly with some rustic, flower-filled urns in an entry. Stencil a wood floor with a border of simple flowers in a darker stain. Paint blooms on canvas floor-cloth or lay a "rug" of Moorish-style floral tiles—clever as well as utilitarian. If a stairway leads up from the entry, glaze the risers in bas-relief tulip tiles or intricate Spanish flower motifs, or choose a carpet that seems to spill flowers down to the door.

bottom left *Flowers don't need to match. Achieve a harmonious whole by grouping items similar in theme or color. Soft light and space for keys take care of practicalities. A cat is optional.*

bottom right *Splurge and cover a wall with "solid wallpaper," slabs of reclaimed building materials painted or printed with large-scale floral designs, like "McGegan Rose" on green marble or "Grand Thistle" on granite.*

Color Gives a Room Ambience and Life

Color creates mood, defines space, and adds decoration. If you're tired of tan or gray and timid about branching out into unexplored color realms, let flowers help you. Soon you'll be living in a blooming bouquet of your own design.

- Gather a bouquet of flowers in your favorite colors (in your garden, at a florist, or from color photographs in a flower catalog). Add and subtract until you have a combination you like. Pull out one shade for the basis of your color scheme and accent with the others.
- Treat your room like a big bouquet with each element a "flower"—a niche of pure color.
- Nature's neutral is green. Its shades are infinite, and there isn't a flower that doesn't go with it. If green isn't your thing, don't worry. Any neutral shade will harmonize with flower colors, too.
- Distribute accent colors to move the eye from one point of interest to another. A garden of flowers all the same height is monotonous, and the same is true for color in your rooms.
- Relax. Mother Nature doesn't care if neighboring colors match exactly, and you shouldn't either.

OTHER FACTORS TO THINK ABOUT WHEN CONSIDERING COLOR

- **Consistency**—Choose a uniform scheme of three colors and you'll be amazed at the patterns and textures you can combine to achieve a pleasing effect.
- **Context**—Look at the setting, the light, and the nearby colors, all of which affect your color choices. Greenish blue seems cool until you set it by hot pink; suddenly it's tropical and warm.
- **Collect**—Compose an idea board with flower pictures, paint chips, fabric swatches, greeting cards—anything with the shades you like. Live with the combination for a while and look at the colors in morning, afternoon, evening, and artificial light.
- **Connect**—Look beyond "safe" to find colors that affect you viscerally. If you love a bold hue but hesitate to make it your dominant color, confine it to easily changed accessories and trims.

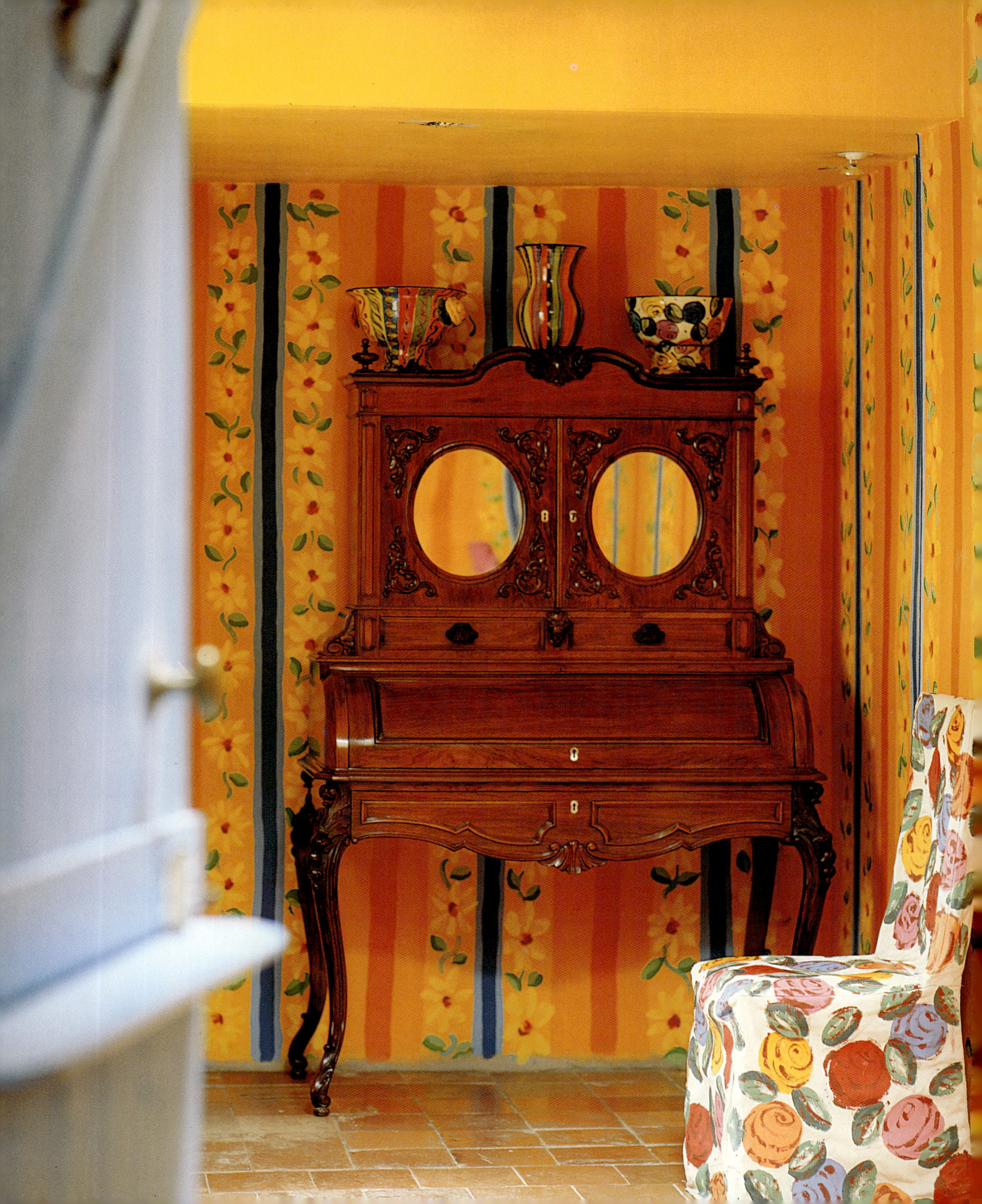

> I have seen a shy young woman completely changed
> because she happened to sit upon a . . . sofa of rose damask.
> I am sure her personality flowered from that hour on.
>
> — Elsie deWolfe

Turn Formulaic into Fun with Flowers

Red, orange, and other strong colors may be too vivid for a whole room, but they're energizing, pleasant, and perfect for an entrance hall where you don't spend a lot of time, and you'll always find flowers to dwell with those hues. Try some faux painting techniques that would be overwhelming in a larger space. Soften an intense or deep color by building up uneven layers of related hues so the walls resemble ancient plaster. Confine the brightest color below a chair rail and paint the top half of the wall a tamer shade to go with flower art and objects. If you can't commit to expanses of rich rose or tiger lily, mount photographs of bright flowers in equally colorful mats to group on the wall. Hang an heirloom quilt of daisies and sunflowers, or tile a wall—or the floor—in bright Italian tiles of filigreed flower patterns.

A plain entry can take a back seat to the accessories. Find or paint a floral frame for a mirror—as showy or subtle as you like. Choose an umbrella stand of metal openwork, a piece of ceramic chinoiserie (Western imitations of Chinese designs), or an old clothes hamper recovered in a bright Hawaiian print. Use a trunk stenciled with tulips as a settee and storage. Put out a beautiful floral tray or glass bowl for keys and loose change. Replace a plain window with stained glass in simple Arts and Crafts roses. No window? Hang a piece of etched or stained glass and light it from behind. Cluster several small botanical prints, toile-painted trays, or floral oil paintings on one wall over a console table holding fresh flowers, or find some unusual flower art, like mosaic collages or laser-cut wooden blooms painted in vibrant colors.

above *Put your entry in the mood with mirrored surfaces, uplighting, and the soft sheen of floral foil wallpaper.*

top *Digital technology opens new floral realms, like the fantastical flower shapes on "Jafleur3" wallpaper, created with photographs of real flower petals that are arranged with the help of a computer.*

opposite *Let your wild side show. You couldn't get away with this riot of color and pattern in a living room, but the combination makes an adventurous statement in a small entry.*

Silk Flowers Aren't Just for Hats Anymore

Anyone who hasn't looked at silk flowers lately is in for a treat. Their variety and lifelike appearance are astounding. What they lack in perfume and palpable sensuality they make up for in versatility and value. They're happy in spots too dimly lit for live plants, can be shaped to suit any arrangement, and will never fade, wilt, or turn brown. Silk flowers have been used for hundreds of years in China and elsewhere to fill in when the real thing wasn't available, and they can do the same for you. Try them as permanent spots of color in any room, to play up a theme, or to draw out the accent colors in fabrics and walls. Here are some ideas to try:

- Craft a small topiary of colorful flowers for a centerpiece. Make a tall one for an entryway.
- Circle a mirror or picture frame with a silk flower wreath.
- Use swags of silk blooms to adorn a doorway, spill flowers down the center of the dining table, or drape them across a mantel.
- Accent the edge of a lampshade, drapery valance, or bedspread with a border of silk flowers. Use them as curtain tie-backs, or sew some onto throw pillows or padded hangers.
- Dress the table for dinner by fashioning silk flowers into napkin rings, tucking one into each napkin, or circling each dinner plate with a bed of flowers. Twine a few in the light fixtures. Open and flatten roses and leaves to make bases for glass votive candleholders.
- Enliven silk flower arrangements with ribbons, real twigs, toys, miniatures, or other trinkets.
- Experiment with containers, since water isn't a concern. Try paper, cardboard, wood, papier-mâché, wicker, wire baskets, or even doll furniture. Glue overlapping silk petals or leaves on a plastic yogurt container.

left *Sprays of flowering branches and a baby grand piano envelop the guests in Old World elegance.*

Choose Classical Motifs for a Formal Floral Look

An entryway untouched by bright sunlight is just the spot to hang a length of painted silk, a medieval garden tapestry, or a square of velvet embroidered with beautiful sprigs. Controlled light protects delicate dyes and adds an elegant touch to the space. Mimic the look of fine fabric hangings with subtle, textured wallpaper like lustrous brocade. Relief wall covering resembles elaborate plasterwork, but it is a durable and washable way to give an entry dado some Art Nouveau lilies or Baroque filigree. Well-positioned lighting will highlight the dimensional designs. Add a frieze of floral-embossed leather to richly crown the room.

Fashion a classical table with a half-moon of glass over a column base. Top it with a neoclassical bronze urn full of deep orange zinnias or a tiered tea stand layered with blooms. Items that once graced grander homes will look just as comfortable in yours. Flea markets and antique shops are full of hidden treasures like ornate mirrors complete with leafy candle sconces, frames carved with rosettes and palmettes, small tables with inlaid floral designs, or consoles draped in Belle Epoque swags. Invite flowers into your entryway and enjoy their company in whatever style you choose.

Flowers through History

The Greeks Preferred Stylized Flowers; Romans Wanted Realism

Twenty-five hundred years ago, the Greeks adapted Egyptian and other floral elements to suit their tastes, perfecting symmetrical ornaments like the *S*-shaped ogees based on the flowers and leaves of water plants. The Greeks also carved bucrania, ox heads often garlanded with flowers, reminders of ancient sacrifices when real ox skulls hung on temple walls. They decorated tombs with irises and wove flowers throughout the myths of their deities. One motif that has stayed popular into the 21st century is the anthemion, a horizontal band of alternating lotus and fan-shaped palmettes.

Rome drew inspiration from Greek and Etruscan sources, but instead of stylized and idealized patterns, the Romans preferred naturalistic scenes of everyday life. Flower-filled gardens were a favorite theme for wall paintings, while Pompeiian wall frescoes bloomed with damask roses. Throughout the Roman Empire, jewel-toned flowers dotted the mosaics of dining rooms, baths, arches, and ceilings in villas. The most opulent used carnelian, jasper, turquoise, and other precious stones to achieve their vibrant color. Nero himself preferred throw pillows stuffed with rose petals. And the many garlands of roses that hung from ceilings gave rise to the phrase *sub rosa*; what was said "beneath the rose" remained confidential. It's no wonder Roman gardeners devoted many acres to roses, even developing ways to heat gardens so they could have roses all year round.

opposite *Gardens and roses were popular motifs for the mosaics that adorned walls and floors in Roman villas. This one, from the early 5th century, shows one way to enjoy a rose garden.*

below *Flowers and classical motifs go together like roses and love. Don't be afraid to mix and match.*

33

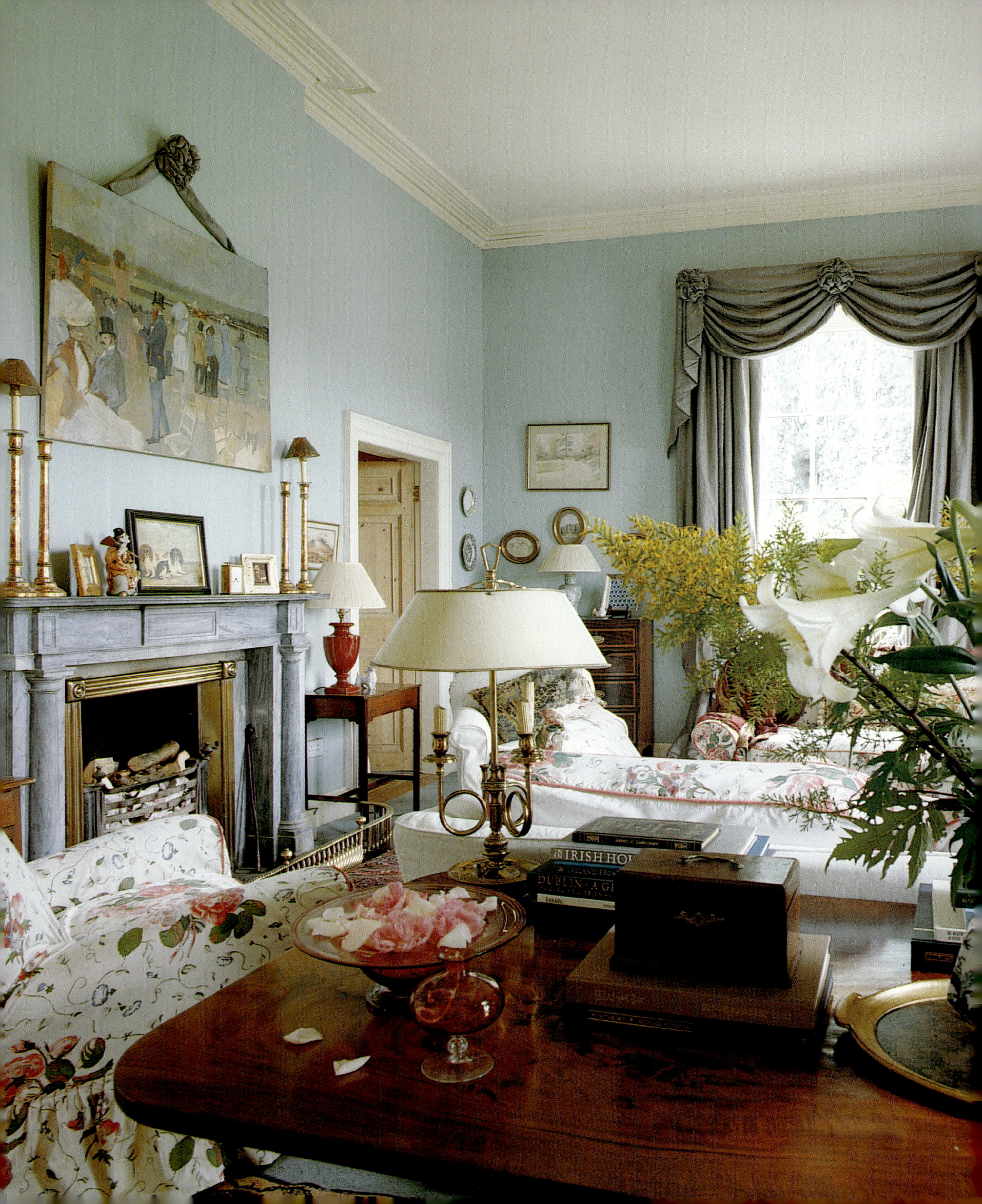

Blooming Living Rooms

Sow hollyhocks and columbines,
The tufted pansy, and the tall
Snapdragon in the broken wall,
Not for this summer, but for next,
Since foresight is the gardener's text

❧ Vita Sackville~West

Do you love chintz inspired by English cottage gardens and glamorously comfortable surroundings? Can you imagine a room awash with soft color and drenched in early morning light that splays in large swaths across a floral Aubusson rug? The light slips past lace-patterned sheers and dances off the walls where Spode plates hang in artful design. At the window, floral-patterned curtains gracefully billow, lifted by a warm breeze. Rose and honeysuckle scent the room. Loosely arranged in a Victorian vase, an armful of old damask and bourbon roses offer a soft touch to the inherited furniture. Their pattern is lavishly repeated in the linens, pillows, and art. An heirloom clock, its face painted a century ago in posies and vines, quietly ticks away the hours in rhythmic cadence. In this room, morning ritual can wait. There's no hurrying the day here. This room beckons you to come feel its embrace.

opposite *Create an indoor English cottage garden with flowers in glorious abundance and myriad forms.*

Create an English Country Room for the Queen in You

You don't have to live in a Cotswold vicarage or a quaint country house in England's Lake District to create an elegant English country ambience in your own living room. With the right combination of colors, fabrics, ornamentation, furniture, and accents, you can transform your current space into an English country escape where you can cavort with your knight, converse with friends, serve afternoon tea, or while away the hours reading works by your favorite author. You need little more than imagination and vision to get started.

Start with the Room's Most Dramatic Natural Focal Point

The natural focal point in the room could be a window with a breathtaking view, ceilings that soar, or a fireplace mantel carved into a stunning rosette. From this feature, move outward into the room, thinking about balance in high and low furniture and the scale of pieces to be used in the room. Also consider traffic patterns and functionality. Then consider interior colors, patterns, and textures. Stick with colors that are soft, mellow, and conducive to a quiet, understated elegance. Draw inspiration from nature's spring/summer palette. Raspberry, rose, and pinks (colors easily found in English cottage gardens filled with fragrant stock, asters, peonies, phlox, and heliotrope) are nicely paired with mint and cream. If you love blues, partner cool delphinium blue with white lily-of-the-valley, or create a warmer palette using the blue of columbine and the yellow of yarrow. For an impressionist look, pair the lavender-blue shade of wisteria with the yellow hue of blooming honeysuckle or the soft purple flowers of fragrant Russian sage with its stalk of gray-blue leaves. Muted tones of gray-blue work well with pale wood to create a quiet space, whereas a brighter intensity of blue or a dusky-hued shade looks best paired with wood of a rich, deep color such as fruitwood, walnut, or mahogany.

Peach is another wonderful color when paired with complementary blue-green. Use these colors in the same low-intensity hue and add yellow-green to the palette to

above What could be a more beautiful or natural focal point than the carved rose and scrollwork on this elegant marble fireplace?

opposite Softly muted shades of color and restrained floral patterns work together to create a quietly elegant look.

complete a soft, but warm and welcoming, décor. Such colors are lovely when used on walls or wood trim and can be further emphasized if they're repeated in the floral patterns in the room. The secret to making two or more colors work in a color scheme is to select colors that are close to the same intensity or purity of color and to keep the value (meaning the lightness or darkness of a color) the same among the two or three colors you choose.

If you prefer wallpaper to paint, there are many options that will project an English country feel. Old patterns of wallpaper are being revived. Use them to cover entire walls or to create a border. Or cut sections of wallpaper and put borders around them to create decorative panels on your walls.

Dress up windows using a chintz pattern and then echo the color in the walls and trim to make them look extraordinary without seeming out of balance with the rest of the room. Or select brocade or heavy velvet in a solid color for drapes and accessorize and accentuate with chintz. Hang curtains from a rod that has decorative floral finials. To really dramatize a window, place a shelf across the wooden rod brackets or add a cornice board to completely hide the rod.

Dramatize with Accent Pieces and Accessories

Use antiques, accessories, and collectibles generously. Antique furniture with a warm wood patina will evoke the feeling of coziness and comfort. Near the fireplace, arrange andirons and tools in pewter, brass, or cast iron. Bring in an old steamer trunk or Victorian hatboxes, or cover plain boxes with floral wallpaper or wrapping paper to hold photos and assorted items within easy reach, but out of sight. Books can go on top. Display collectibles such as Blue Willow, cloisonné, or chintz-ware teapots, petit point or needlepoint pillows depicting pastoral scenes of meadows and flowers, or pressed flowers captured in all their blooming glory in delicate frames. Add some gilded candlesticks. If they look too new, make them look old by applying gold leaf or a paste to age metals. They will look like heirlooms passed down from the lord and lady of the manor to you.

For interest, place a cut-glass, Victorian iron lace-work, or hand-painted ceramic vase on a carved wood coffer, antique chest, or writing desk. Fill the vase with massive blooms of heavily scented old shrub roses and hybrid tea roses. If fresh flowers are not available, substitute silk cabbage roses, hellebores, or peonies. Mix a potpourri of a variety of different colored rose petals, chamomile, and heather with some rose or geranium essential oil. Place it all in a beautiful bowl to scent your English country living room.

Set out a silver, pewter, or china tea service complete with cups and saucers adorned in delicate violas, tuberose, or your favorite flower design. To dress up a wall, consider hanging a slim panel of silk or toile de Jouy fabric onto which you've affixed fabric roses and ribbons at the top and pictures of loved ones in miniature silver frames along its length. Add a tapestry or wall hanging showing the grandeur of an English garden in full bloom or a hunt scene in a meadow of wildflowers. Find and hang prints by Victorian landscape artists who settled in and near Surrey where wildflowers once grew in unspoiled splendor. *Surrey Bluebells*, by John Clayton Adams, and *In the Meadow*, by Edward Wilkins Waite, come to mind. Hang tasseled butler bells or bell pulls in richly colored silk or classic floral patterns adapted from English document fabric. Embellish the garden look by adding Victorian wall or floor tile. Remember that English country style is synonymous with a faded elegance, but it is always comfortable and welcoming. It is a style that you can dress up or down, but most important, it is a style that is easily lived in.

left *This lovely Victorian wall tile featuring an Art Nouveau-style iris in full bloom would be an enchanting accent on a wall that opens out into a garden or transitions to an adjacent room.*

above Hang a bit of wallpaper and add a pair of topiaries along with a couple of rose-covered armchairs and you've got a wee bit of the countryside in any room of the house. Don't forget the doggie pillow.

left Lovebirds perched on the rim of a bowl of potpourri next to a Victorian vase of roses, picked at the height of perfection, will add a romantic softness to any room.

Blooming Living Rooms 39

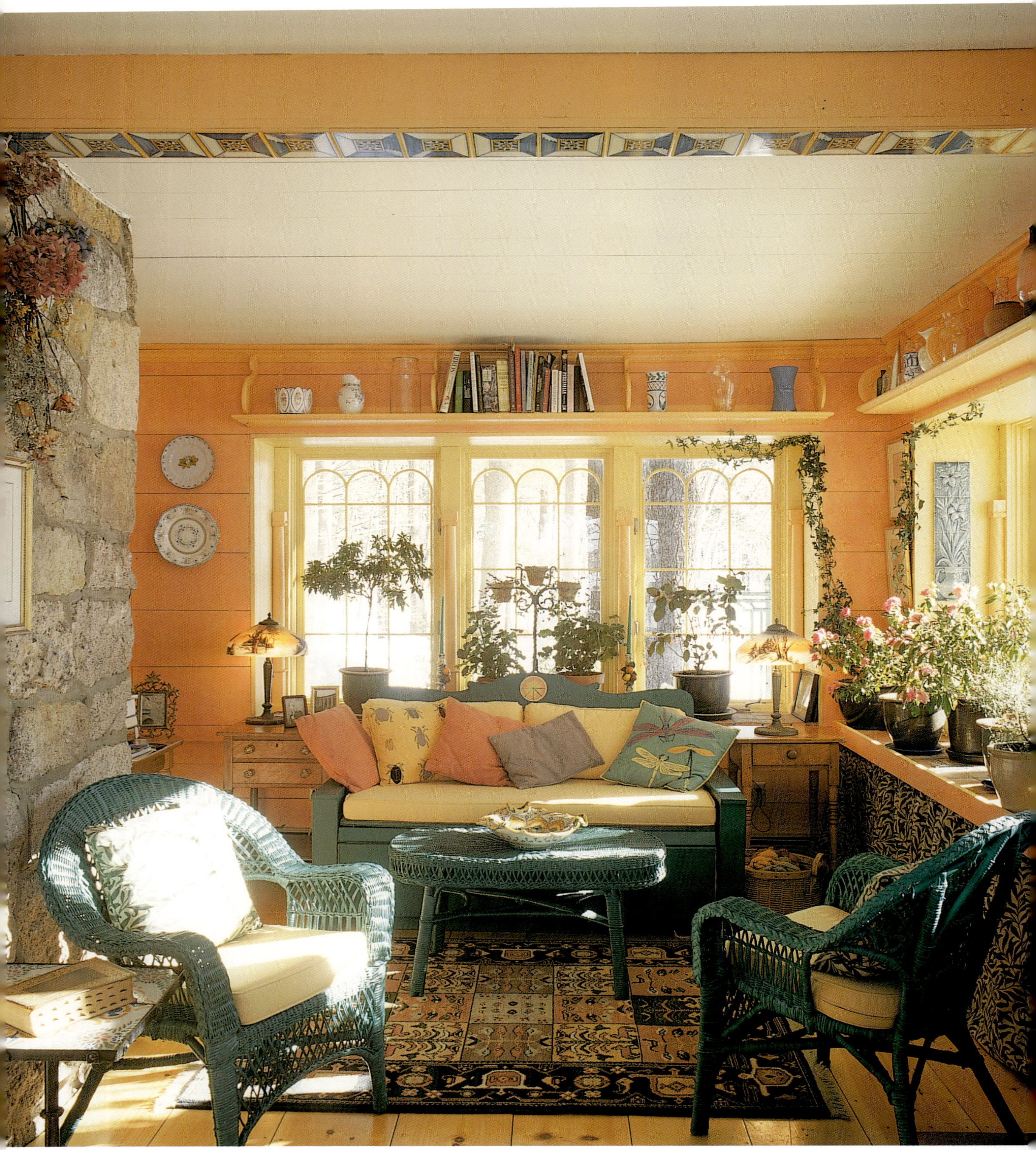

Transform Castoffs into Clever Country Chic

If the English country and antique look isn't your style, but peonies, painted porches, flea market finds, and wicker are, then you may feel more at home in a room with earthier charms and a nostalgic rural feeling. Regardless of the part of the world where you find this style, there is timelessness about it. It hearkens back to earlier, hardworking generations of people who were frugal, self-sufficient, and family-centric. Their homes featured a rustic and utilitarian appeal, and you sensed that a cup of coffee and a slice of pie were waiting just for you.

Capitalize on Farmhouse Collectibles and Other Treasures

To create your country chic living room, take stock of your collection of farmhouse castoffs, flea-market treasures, and garage sale finds to consider how you might use them. Which ones need repair, paint, nails, and screws to be functional once again? Do you have any chairs with grass, reed, or cane seats or furniture pieces made of bent twig? If so, think of ways to incorporate their rustic charm in the décor. Update other old furniture with paint and patterns drawn from flora indigenous to rural places. Furniture painted with popular motifs of fruit, flowers, herbs, grasses, and vegetables looks great and adds character and interest to any room in which it is placed. Use a pie safe or jelly cabinet with punched tin doors, classic farmhouse tables and benches, and lots of shelves. If you own a coffee table of wicker or pine, consider having a piece of glass cut to protect the top. Under the glass, place old flower seed packets. Braided and hand-loomed rugs go well in this kind of interior.

Country chic style is often characterized by painted wicker, generously sized floral pillows, scrubbed and waxed pine furniture, colorful pottery, dried bunches of herbs and flowers, stamped, stenciled, or painted decorations on walls (and sometimes floors and other surfaces), printed cottons, quilted fabrics, and assorted collectibles. But it is with the use of wall covering and color that the room begins to really come alive. Think about incorporating wildflowers, such as bluebonnets and poppies found along highways and byways, or cultivated flowers like black-eyed Susans, giant sunflowers, and hollyhocks, since these have long been associated with country and farms.

Create a Purely Country Color Scheme

Color makes a huge impact, so carefully consider what palette might work best with your furnishings. Are the colors you most love the ones you could live with, or do you just like visiting them from time to time? Try your colors on paper first and walk them through the room. Consider how the light from windows, skylights, and doors might move through the room over these colors during the daylight hours.

above Sunflowers and an old metal basin are perfectly paired in this quiet corner.

opposite The summer garden colors of gold, orange, yellow, and green warm and dramatize the natural materials of stone, wood, and wicker in this room.

Do bold, bright primary colors like red, blue, and yellow excite you? Or do you prefer ethereal pastels and muted tones? If you love farmhouse checks of red and white with accents in blue, give it a try. But don't rule out other options. What if you used a tone-on-tone combination of the sunny yellows that might be found in zinnias, marigolds, and yarrow? Then add a dash of red-lavender (think of gloxinia or bunches of lilacs in a slightly redder hue). These colors will combine for a visually exciting and energetic palette. Then, for balance, add a green-turquoise and a soft shade of periwinkle blue used in plaid to cover cushions for straight-back chairs. Pick up the colors in a floral pattern for sofa cushions and window treatments. Finally, incorporate the color scheme in embroidered table linens. Coordinate your colors in braided rag rugs, or choose hand-woven rugs that feature country flowers in full bloom.

Wallpaper is always changing to meet the tastes of home decorators. Capitalize on the renewed interest in vintage papers with authentic floral designs. Apply stripes a third of the way up the wall and paste coordinating florals from the top of the striped wallpaper to the ceiling. Where the two pieces meet, paste a border over the seam. Or consider covering your walls using a combination of painting and stenciling. For example, stencil a chair rail around the room in a flowery, folksy pattern; then paint above and below. Painting techniques include combing, rag rolling, spattering, sponging, stippling, or dry brushing. Use the style that most appeals to you.

Don't like paint? Fabrics of all kinds have been used since the beginning of time to cover walls for aesthetic purposes and to conserve warmth. Consider using quilts as wall art. Think of ways to play off different traditional patterns and colors.

opposite *A painted wooden cupboard with decorative trim can hold Grandma's mixing bowls, old pottery, or a collection of quilting fabric in a country chic interior. The red and white tulips echo the floral patterns in the room.*

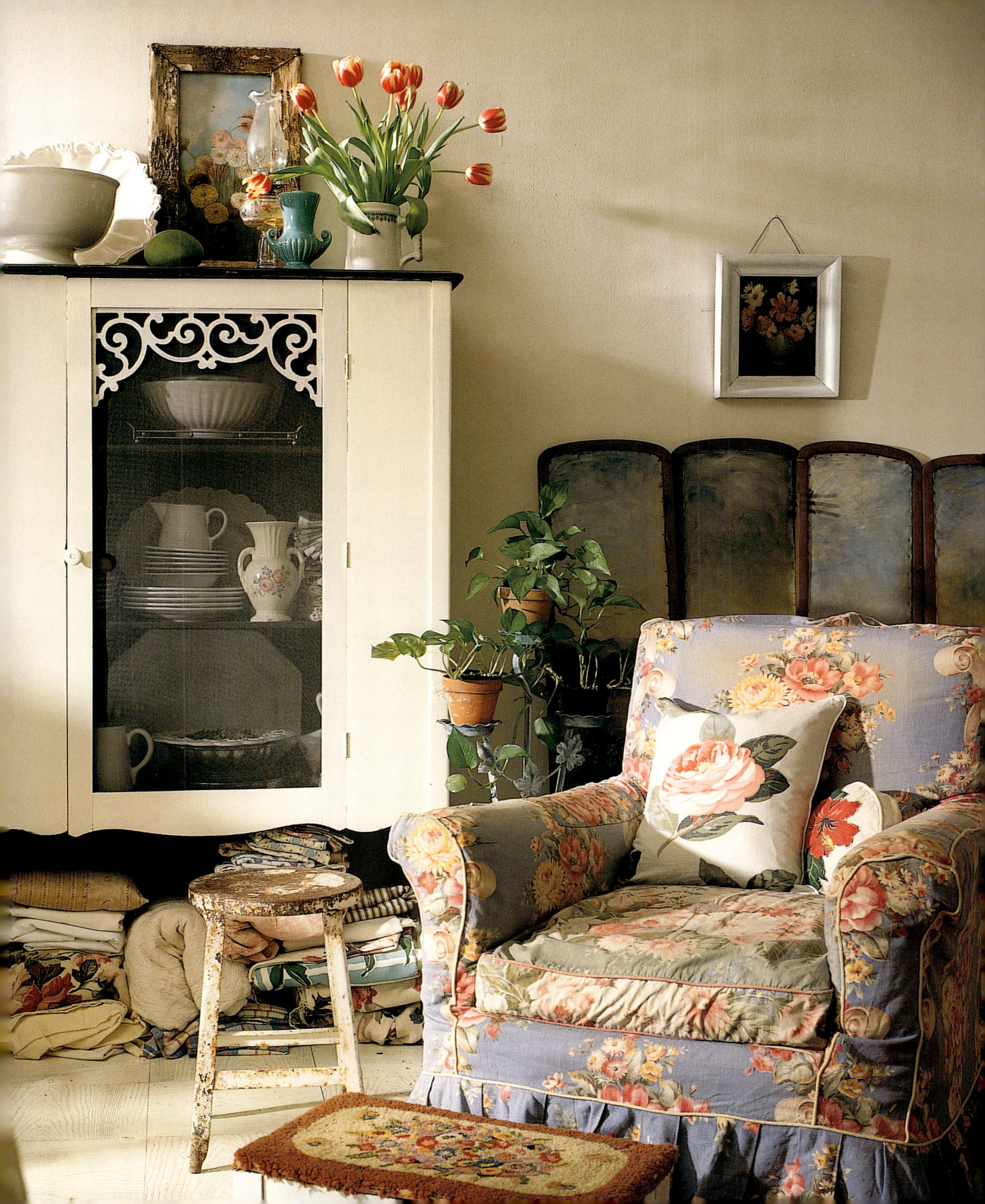

above *Taking cues from the bouquet, the coordinated fabrics of the furniture and pillows create focal points of bright color in an otherwise dark library.*

Group Baskets, Folk Art, or Farm Implements

Accessorize the room with country-themed utilitarian objects, art, baskets, and lots of greenery. Scour antique stores and rural thrift stores for vintage products and collectibles. Lampshades pinpricked in the motif of hearts and flowers that were commonly found in Shaker and American folk art add an authentic touch to the American country look of a room.

Recycle barn boards or use new wood to make shelves. Paint or leave them natural and group similar types of country collectibles on the shelves. Consider items like these:

- Birdhouses
- Ceramic or carved wooden farm animals
- Weathervanes
- Thimble collections
- Old embroidery hoops
- Farm implements such as old saws, buckets, watering cans, and egg baskets
- Dishware and farmhouse kitchen culinary tools such as rolling pins, flour sifters, old mixing bowls, and wooden spoons
- American country metal-ware and bowls, pottery crocks, and pitchers with matching bowls
- Old fruit crates with labels
- Tin boxes, old irons, and beautiful old glass

If you can find them, children's toys made of paper or wood (playing cards, miniature telephones, paper dolls, cars and tractors, books), as well as child-size furniture, add wonderful country touches. Paint old picture frames white and group them together. Insert keepsake family photos, farm scenes, or black-and-white prints of farmers during the Depression. On the top of a rustic coffee table, place images cut from paper that show aspects of rural life (farmers and flowers seem to always go together), or try vintage floral valentines, packages of heirloom flower seed, or collectible postcards with botanical images. Cover the top of the coffee table with glass to protect the paper items. Decorate an old chest in the Pennsylvania German art that incorporates beautiful designs of flowers grown in early American gardens. Float seasonal water lilies in rustic enamel basins or tubs.

above A stunning floral arrangement, coupled with matching blue-and-white ceramics stand before a folk art screen with panels depicting everyday scenes of country life.

Over panels of finely woven cotton curtains, hang buttoned valances in country flower patterns. For the buttons, choose sunflower-shaped buttons or make miniature fabric roses. Or feed a pretty floral topper with a wide casing along a simple pole and affix ribbon-tied bunches of dried flowers at intervals across the top. Make long cotton curtains country cute with the addition of sunflower tiebacks. Don't be afraid to stamp upon this room the impression of your country chic sensibility and style.

Follow Crisp, Clean Lines to an Asian Sensibility

Think of a room that feels Asian or Oriental in design. Do you picture open, high-ceiling rooms with lots of wall space decorated in 18th-century Chinese wallpaper complete with lacquered panels, Chinese pilasters, fretwork, and friezes? Are the carpets sumptuous and elegantly adorned in the colors of delicate flowers, and are those floral colors and shapes echoed in candles, fabrics, furniture, and the architecture of the room? Are there shiny surfaces everywhere, along with an obvious but judicious use of gold, silver, and other metals in the ornamentation of cabinetry, lamps, and the like? This room hearkens back to a bygone era, and you would likely need ample space to create a similar feeling. But such an interior could be created through the use of chinoiserie and Oriental ornamentation in pictures, porcelain, fabrics, furniture, lamps, statuary, and all sorts of containers. Don't forget flowers. Dramatic blooming orchids in brilliant colors and complex shapes would add an interesting dimension to this type of room.

Integrate the Symbolic Elements of Feng Shui

You can easily create another type of room with an Asian feel by utilizing the principles of feng shui. The art of feng shui draws upon nature's own elements and uses them in rooms in ways designed to bring good fortune and happiness into the home. Specifically, there are five elements: water, fire, wood, earth, and metal. Think of the natural elements you find in the following: a tree-lined glade, a marsh of wild grass, the shoals of a lazy river, a narrow stream gurgling over moss-covered stones, and a mountain ridge turned blue by twilight. You've probably figured out that the colors are primarily neutral, while textures, shapes, and structures are varied. Colors like white, gold, and silver, for example, and round shapes represent metal, while green and brown, along with rectangular shapes, represent the wood element. Red, of course, represents fire, but so do yellow and orange and pointed or triangular shapes. Beige, light yellow, and mocha hues quite naturally represent earth. Water—as you can guess—is represented by wavy lines (the ancient symbol for water) and the colors of blue and black. It is also interesting to note that flat, smooth surfaces allow a rapid flow of energy, whereas rough textures impede that flow.

The first thing to consider as you plan out this room is how to bring in these five elements of nature and incorporate their symbolism in colors, textures, shapes, and structures. Stick to quiet neutrals for wall color. Keep design lines clean. Get rid of all clutter. Coordinate the scale of furniture to the size of the room to achieve a harmonic balance. Make generous use of natural materials, including rattan, bamboo, wood, wicker, clay, stone, glass, and metal in floor coverings, built-ins, bases, furniture, and moldings. Choose soft furnishings from a selection of natural fibers like cotton, wool, silk, or linen.

Subtle energies, according to ancient Chinese teachings, are moving through your home, your body, and the entire universe at all times. The goal of a feng shui room is to ensure that the energy is working for you, not against you. Ideally, if all elements of the room are correctly positioned, you are likely to have a positive mental outlook and feelings of well-being whenever you are in this room. Creating this type of room can feel a little daunting, but if it's something you really want to do, you'll find there are many resources available to help you through the process.

Balance Yin and Yang Using Floral Motifs

Practitioners of feng shui believe that the energy in a room can be altered by the choice and placement of furniture, color, synthetic fibers, building materials, artificial lighting, and flowers. This energy will be either yin (passive) or yang (active). Muted, soft hues are yin, for example, while bold, bright colors are yang. When incorporating flowers into such an Asian interior, first consider the pattern. Is it large or small? What is the significance of the flower's color and type? Will you use the image in curtains, for pillow

left *There is no competition for the view in this quiet space where flowers hang from the ceiling in a collection of lovely lanterns.*

coverings, in a rug, or as part of an accent such as the frame of mirror? Perhaps you'll use your flowers in a massive watercolor print, a decorative screen, or a customized, painted accent around a window. Maybe you'll do nothing more than add a perfect single specimen of your favorite flower to a vase that's anchored to a wall by a metal sconce.

Remember that a feng shui interior is rich in symbolic detail. Flowers and plants are one of those details. For fresh flowers, always choose fewer, more magnificent and elegant blooms rather than lots of extravagant and exotic flowers, and no spiny cactus. Keep floral arrangements simple, yet dramatic—a dab of pink from peonies (to bring romance), a touch of purple from irises, a splash of fuchsia from a blooming orchid. In stark contrast to English and American country and the more ornate Asian styles, this type of interior is most beautiful when flowers, judiciously chosen, are thoughtfully displayed. For example, put an exquisite rosebud with a long stem in a clear vase, a single perfect camellia blossom in a bowl, or a handful of pussy willows or cattails in a tall, cylindrical, hand-thrown pot.

Peace lilies or the lucky bamboo plant, depending on their placement in a room, can thwart negative energy and promote a feeling of peacefulness. To add fire energy to a room, add a dinner-plate-size dahlia in a tall thin vase.

Beyond Chintz
UNUSUAL FLORAL PATTERNS AND FLOWERS FOR EVERY TASTE

Designers create floral motifs for home and garden accents, textiles, and furniture from the most popular and best-known varieties of flowers for a good reason—to appeal to the broadest possible audience. Among the plethora of popular floral choices are poppy, daisy, geranium, sunflower, hibiscus, hollyhock, hydrangea, iris, tulip, petunia, lily, wisteria, and everyone's favorite, the rose. Even Old Masters and modern artists often painted the common flowers. For example, consider Van Gogh's *Sunflowers* and *Irises*; Georgia O'Keeffe's *Black and Purple Petunias* and *White Camellia*; Claude Monet's *Sunflowers*, *Wild Poppies Near Argenteuil*, and *Water Lilies*; and Diego Rivera's *Vendedora de Alcatraces* (which shows a woman dwarfed by three enormous bunches of calla lilies). But why not be daring and try working out your own unusual pairings of patterns and prints from the list of ten ideas offered here.

left *This fanciful stool by Nicole Chazaud Telaar for Festive Fibers illustrates a refreshingly creative approach to pattern and color.*

opposite *White recedes and makes the perfect foil for old and unusual pieces of furniture, a chorus of brightly colored and patterned pillows, and a one-of-a-kind chandelier.*

- Combine festive, incongruous patterns. Mix plaids with florals and solids and integrate the three different patterns with the same color palette.
- Mix shapes. Pair geometric designs with floral borders or use bold floral patterns with two-tone vines (and they don't have to be green).
- Integrate patterns of small buds on trailing vines with lavish, ultra-large flowers in the style of Georgia O'Keeffe.
- Use abstract designs in bold colors with mini-prints of delicate ornamental annuals.
- Place retro tropical floral patterns with aquatic or animal motifs.
- Mix paisley with stripes, using the same colors in similar values.
- Combine African safari prints with arabesque floral shapes.
- Mix medieval floral ornamentation with Celtic knot patterns.
- Use diagonal or diamond patterns with ornate ovals featuring Art Nouveau flowers and leaves.
- Consider incorporating floral ornamentation in two patterns that are the reverse of each other.

BEYOND THE EASEL
Sargent
MATERIAL WORLD
BONNARD
Jonathan Miller
WILFRED THESIGER

right *Spruce up the end of a hall or plain wall with a unique piece of furniture and a splash of color echoed in flowers.*

Put out some brilliant red branches of the Coral Embers willow in an angular metal container. Red blooms of pansies and tulips can add fire color in the spring; begonias, cannas, and gladiola work for summer; and chrysanthemums and some species of Oriental poppies in the fall can also "awaken" the fire element in a room, especially if the room has no wood stove or fireplace. Just remember to throw out flowers as soon as they begin to look faded; you don't want "dead or dying" energy in the room. For that reason, do not use dried flowers in this type of space.

Another idea for using flowers in their many incarnations in this type of room is to incorporate antique Chinese porcelain vases or reproductions with delicate floral images or use prints or posters of the blossoming branches of fruit trees or berries. Find a strategic location and move in a lacquered chest painted with flowers and Chinese calligraphy. In a room with a lot of yang (or male) energy, add circular shapes that are yin (feminine). For example, place some ceramic balls with blue-and-white floral designs in a reed basket or float a magnolia bloom in a clear glass bowl. According to the art of feng shui, your efforts will pay big dividends in excellent health, positive thinking, and an increase in wealth, harmony, happiness, and well-being.

Evoke Ethnic Style with Cultural Colors and Floral Patterns

The ethnic style we've chosen to explore is Indian; however, many of the ideas that follow apply just as easily to an African, Moroccan, or Tunisian ethnic style, among many others. The point is to find objects, textiles, shapes, patterns, furniture, and colors that evoke images of a particular culture and to use them in creating an interior enhanced with all those elements.

To travel to India is to enter a world pulsating with a riot of color, a cacophony of sounds, tantalizing tactile sensations, and exotic scents. Living rooms here are as diverse as the people who inhabit them. Indian interiors, however, might best be characterized by a lavish use of color and by furnishings in natural fibers and fabrics, with the judicious accompaniment of shimmering mirrors, gold and silver thread, and patterns and ornamentation evocative of the flora and fauna found on the hot Indian subcontinent.

Floral ornamentation, both ancient and modern, adorns Indian textiles, floor tiles, stonework, fretwork, furniture, and architecture and seems to be an organic part of the whole. Flowers are found on embroidered and woven fabrics, including cashmere shawls in colorful paisley patterns based on an ancient teardrop Persian motif. Though woven in India, these shawls, with their soft fabric and delicate designs, which often include flowers as part of the pattern, were much sought after in 18th-century France and even captured the fancy of royalty. Empress Josephine, pictured in an oil painting by Antoine-Jean Gros, is seen wearing a dress made of a long Kashmir paisley shawl with a dramatic and different orange shawl draped over her shoulder.

Other beautiful examples of Indian floral motifs may be found on Indian chintzes (from the Hindi word *chint*). These floral fabrics have been in demand in Britain and Europe since the 16th century, when Queen Elizabeth granted a charter to English merchants to begin trade with India. The East India Company introduced printed or painted Indian cotton wall hangings, called *palampores*, to England, and these in turn inspired British artists. The highly stylized floral designs must have also curried favor with English ladies, because many women began incorporating into their projects these renderings of flowers common to ancient tree-of-life patterns.

Make Liberal Use of Indian Floral Motifs

India's love affair with the flower is evident in exquisite silk sari borders and handmade rugs. Floral motifs are also found on cabinets, wood mirrors, and lacquered boxes. Throughout the subcontinent, you will find such ornamentation in the spandrel of an arch, the column of a centuries-old temple, the wooden door of a public building, or a wooden panel for a *zenana*. During the Moghul rule in India, women were segregated into an area known as a *zenana*. From this place in a home or palace, they could view the outside world through panels of intricately carved (almost lacelike) windows. The panel carvers were inspired by images of trees and flowers and freely incorporated these images in their delicate carvings.

How do you use the floral designs, shapes, and colors of the Indian subcontinent to create your very own ethnic space? Begin with a neutral, but warm, wall color. Soft tones of marigold, zinnia, saffron, and even the lightest blush of rose serve as a quiet foil for brightly colored pillows, curtains, and floor coverings in turmeric orange, pomegranate red, indigo blue, eggplant purple, sap green, and nutmeg brown. The black of the Indian mustard seed works as a stunning accent color, as do shades of lemony yellow. Amber, straw, and white work well as base colors for seat cushions.

Choose furniture made of stone, wood, or metal in interesting shapes with eye-catching embellishments (intricate carvings of flora and fauna or inlaid mother-of-pearl are popular). Or select furniture pieces made of cane—first introduced to Britain and Europe by the East India Company in the 17th century. Plan on having one or more low tables on which to place a flower press; herbal, gardening, and travel books; carved art; and a highly polished brass bowl to hold fruit or fresh flowers. Add a long divan, sofa, or futon and cover it with a durable fabric in the color of curd, linen, terra cotta, or sandalwood.

Since luxurious fabrics soften the sharp edges and angular shapes of the furniture, add a sumptuous silk quilt or Indian block-print throw in a warm hue that harmonizes well with the wall color. Finish off with satiny pillows in the rich colors of eggplant, cherry, mango, lime, and pink—colors that stand up well against the searing bright sunlight of the subcontinent as well as the neutral hues of your living room walls and seat cushions. If you make the

There were roses in the hedges, and sunshine in the sky,
Red lilies in the sedges, where the water rippled by,
A thousand bulbuls singing, oh, how jubilant they were,
And a thousand flowers flinging their sweetness on the air.

—Anonymous, from *India's Love Lyrics*

pillows yourself, decorate them with flowers—red lotus (which stands for Mother India), marigolds, chrysanthemums, or roses—embroidered, stamped, or appliquéd. Create the shapes of flowers using beads and sew them into the fabric. Or cover pillow forms with some version of the "Arborescent Indienne" toile de Jouy pattern that was itself designed from the *palampores*.

The arch is a common architectural element in India and is widely used to frame doors, windows, and verandas. Create the illusion of an arch by loosely hanging panels of gossamer cotton across the ceiling—cotton that, according to Brinda Gill writing in *India Perspective*, was once called by such evocative names as "running water," "night dew," and "woven air" to indicate its degree of fineness. If there is ample wall space, consider creating a trompe l'oeil element, perhaps a delicate scalloped arch sitting atop two pillars. Embellish the arch with flowers, elephants, fruits, monkeys, trees, and other ethnic motifs. Or simply add a wooden stand-alone screen—try to find one with panels that are shaped in arches at the top. Drape over the screen a swath of glamorous silk embellished in the rose or lotus shapes common in India or adorned with gold or silver sequins and thread. If you prefer, hang a richly colored paisley shawl or a roughly textured blanket of bold patterns that mimic those popular among India's indigenous tribal people.

If your living room has tile or hardwood floors, put down some natural fiber coir mats (made from coconut husk fibers), dhurries (Indian cotton rugs), or jute or rush mats to soften the look, define sitting areas, and warm the room. Imported prints of miniature Moghul paintings, soapstone carvings and folk art from Indian villages, or blue pottery water pitchers and flower vases from Jaipur add visual interest. Place scented candles in pottery or brass candlestick holders and strategically position them where they will add a delicate floral scent and a soft light. Wall hangings of tie-dyed silk from India's Gujarat state or the embroidery and mirror work so typical of India's Rajasthani villages provide a dramatic finishing touch. A vibrant cloth painting or wall hanging decorated with cowrie shells would also work. Finally, display bunches of marigolds, geraniums, chrysanthemums, gardenias, or roses—flowers commonly found throughout India—in highly polished brass pots.

above *A fringed curtain in auspicious red (often the preferred color for a wedding sari) unifies disparate patterns in this ethnic-inspired interior.*

Blooming Ideas

HOW TO PRINT YOUR OWN FLORAL WALLPAPER OR FABRICS

There are several methods for creating beautiful images on walls or fabrics. Here are a few ideas to get you started. Caveat: For best results, you'll want to use fabric paint for stamping or painting onto cloth. Another option for making beautiful flowers on cloth is to use fabric dyes (especially on silk). However, if you are not already familiar with the steps involved in dyeing fabric using direct dyes, acid dyes, fiber-reactive dyes, and natural dyes and pigments, you might want to consult one or more of the excellent books available on this topic.

- **Decoupaging**—Use decoupage paste to attach a pretty garden border directly onto a painted wall. Find old valentines or other floral cards, prints, engravings, or even embossed or raised flowers on old stationery (that can be cut out and painted—watercolors would be lovely) and use them to create a blooming border around doorways, along baseboards, or over an alcove.

- **Freehand painting**—Create a trailing vine up a wall, across the top and down the sides of a window, or above an arched entrance to a room.

- **Papering with homemade paper**—Make your own paper or buy rolls of butcher paper or craft paper and stencil, paint, or stamp floral designs or create and attach delicate flowers made from tissue. Hang your work like wallpaper. Or purchase sheets of beautiful handmade paper (with bits of flower petals and leaves). Hang this as is, or paint, stamp, or stencil floral images or glue petals of dried flowers onto the paper before attaching it to the wall.

- **Stamping**—Use a stamp with a floral design. Place guide marks everywhere you want an image to appear on the wall or fabric. Then, using pretty paints or inks, stamp your flower design randomly or in a set pattern across a wall.

- **Stenciling**—Paint a flower pattern right where you want it, using a stencil made from acetate or plastic. To make your own stencil, find a floral image you like. Place acetate, plastic, or transparency paper over it and outline the image onto the acetate using a felt-tip pen. Using a crafter's knife or scissors, cut out the parts of the image that will be painted on the wall or onto fabric. For walls, make the stencil long enough that the pattern repeats at least three times. Adding graceful stems, tendrils, buds, and leaves by hand can turn an ordinary flower border into a lush, ornate work of Art Nouveau.

above Pluck a pattern from the wall and pick it up in pillows and painted furniture

Flowers through History

Asian Artisans Created Realistic and Symbolic Flower Embellishments

By the end of the first millennium, China was making extensive and exquisite use of flowers in every sort of decorative art. Realistic orchids, roses, and jasmine sprouted on fabrics, boxes, screens, ceramics, and furniture.

Japanese artisans borrowed Chinese and Korean traditional motifs and gave them an asymmetrical twist, reveling in the shapes of cherry blossom twigs, peonies, and camellias while highlighting the unique qualities of each individual flower. They perfected the art of enameling flower decorations onto glazed porcelain. When fired a second time, the rhododendrons and other blooms shimmered with deep, rich color. From the inlaid lead and mother-of-pearl irises and chrysanthemums on writing boxes to the plum-blossom openwork on hanging lanterns or the draping wisteria on tea-leaf storage jars, Japanese decoration celebrated the intricate glory of flowers.

Many Indian Floral Patterns Have Survived Virtually Unchanged

Centuries of ornamentation in India featured simple repetition, profuse patterns, and warm harmonious colors, with decoration filling every inch of a textile or object. Bright pink, blue, and white water lilies inspired architectural elements, including the now-familiar rosette, as well as palmettes intertwined with leaves and tendrils. Elaborately carved cabinetry, often inlaid with mother-of-pearl or ivory, featured intricate floral designs. Painted lacquer work might depict a tall vase overflowing with richly hued blooms.

Exported Indian cotton fabric was wildly popular in the 17th century. Called calico because it came from Calicut, these textiles were painted or printed in bold florals and other patterns, and their appeal has endured to this day. The Victorians couldn't get enough Indian cotton chintz, especially the "flowering tree" pattern, and many of the floral designs are still available.

❊ ❊ ❊ ❊ ❊ ❊ ❊ ❊ ❊ ❊ ❊ ❊ ❊

opposite *One can almost smell the peonies on these 19th-century Korean screens of joshi (cotton, silk, and hemp fabric).*

top *Delicate floral tracery adorns this 18th-century chintz palampore, or coverlet, from India's Coromandel Coast.*

center *A leaf from an 18th-century Indian book of designs for textiles.*

bottom *This ethnic interior, with its exuberant pairing of softly illuminated colors, patterned fabrics, and textural elements, suggests a place of enchantment where one could easily forget about time and worldly obligations.*

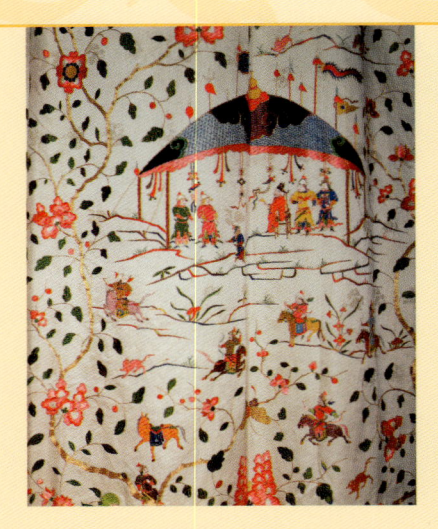

55

Blooming Kitchens

China tea, the scent of hyacinths, wood fires, and bowls of violets— that is my mental picture of an agreeable February afternoon.

— Constance Spry

Of all the rooms in the house, the kitchen demands a certain level of functionality. Surfaces need to be durable, washable, and capacious enough for meal preparation. Light needs to be bright and well positioned. Food storage and appliances are a given. There is usually an area large enough for eating as well. But can you think of another room in which you are less likely to take a nap? All the rules about subdued, calming tones for bedrooms or living rooms can fly right out the kitchen window. Here is the spot for glorious sunflower or eye-popping petunia. Whether you put the flowers in the food, on the walls, or in the accessories, a kitchen is made to bloom.

❀ ❀ ❀ ❀ ❀ ❀ ❀ ❀ ❀ ❀ ❀ ❀ ❀ ❀ ❀

opposite *Not using the stove right now? Cover it with vases full of seasonal flowers, and turn a humdrum kitchen meal into a picnic.*

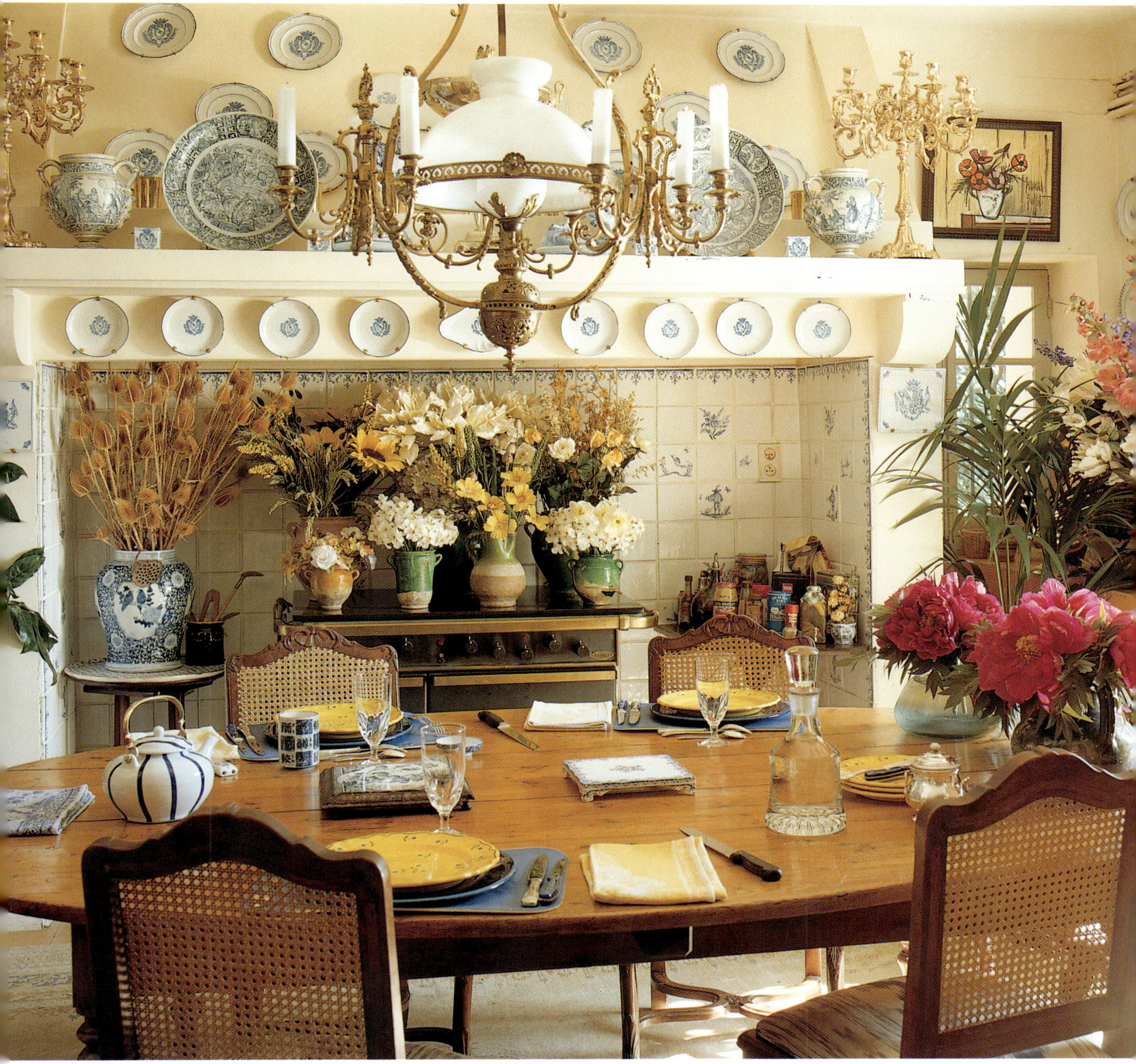

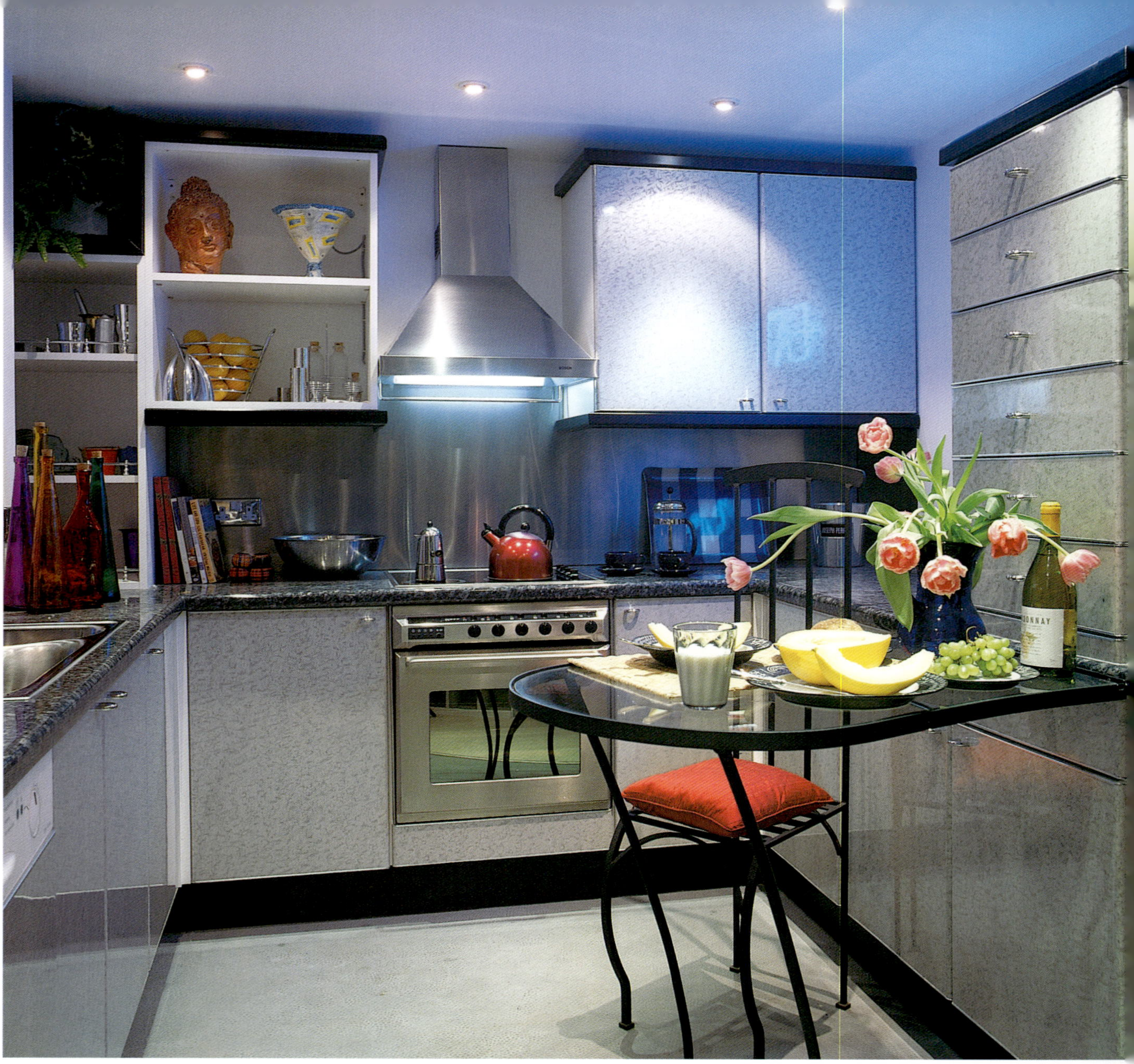

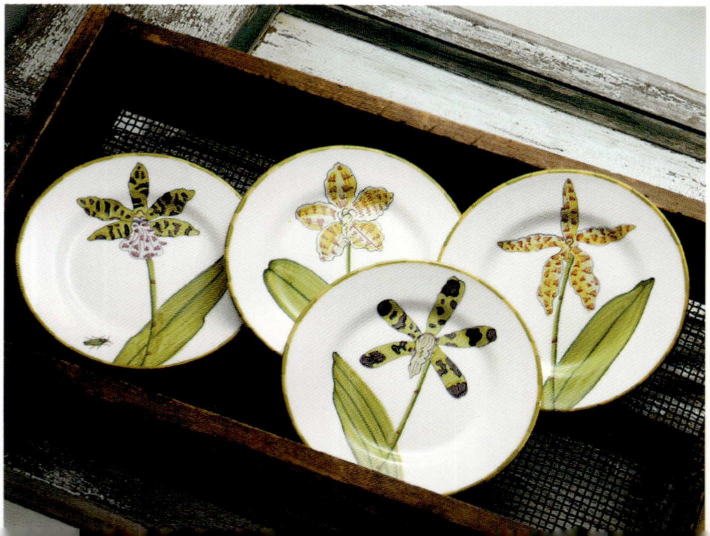

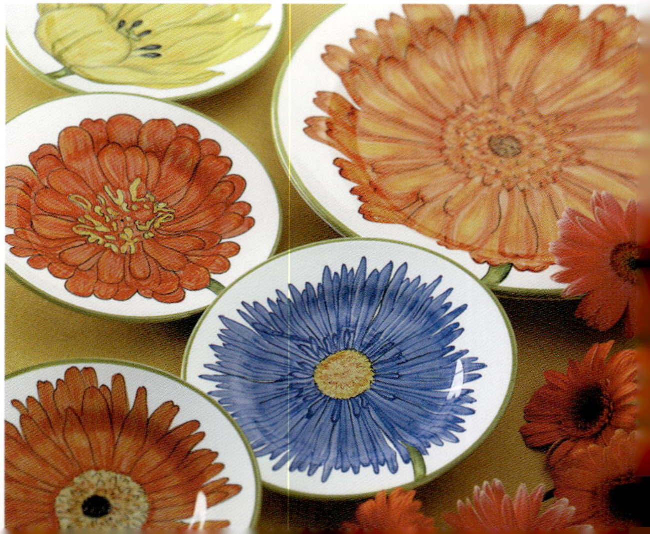

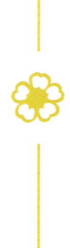

Balance Kitchen Technology with the Softness and Color of Blooms

Today's kitchens are brimful of high-tech appliances, surfaces impervious to stains, and flooring that can withstand the heavy traffic of kids and pets. But even with concessions to practicality, you can add plenty of sophisticated or surprising floral motifs to the room.

Red stimulates the appetite, which is probably why there aren't many red refrigerators around. But what cayenne pepper is to cooking, a dash of hot color is to a kitchen, adding zip especially to windowless or north-facing rooms. Plenty of styles embrace flowers in warm palettes. Try fabrics from Provence, Tuscan pottery, Mexican furniture, or Spanish tiles. Wake up the walls in a retro-1950s or gentler 1940s floral. Old designs are being re-issued in durable materials, and you can still find rolls of original papers for sale at specialty shops.

If you prefer your walls a solid color, line open shelves with floral paper or curtain the insides of glass- or chicken-wire-paneled doors. Give the backsplash its own floral twist—look through architectural salvage stores for carved stone flowers or old, tin ceiling panels of rosettes or other patterns. Today there are even wallpapers that replicate the look of old tin ceilings and are made to be painted. If you have floral china or serving pieces that are too pretty to keep behind closed doors, add a shelf near the ceiling where you can store and show off pitchers, vases, bowls, and other items not needed every day.

Put the Fun Back in Functional with Flowers

Flowers have long been welcome in the dining room, where fresh arrangements, elegant floral fabrics, and fine porcelain with delicately painted blossoms have reigned for hundreds of years. Bring more playful blooms for everyday use into the kitchen, where formality takes a back seat to efficiency.

Floral motif tiles have proliferated as rapidly as flowers in May. Enliven the backsplash or a drab corner of the counter with a mosaic of tiles realistically painted to look like an overflowing vase of flowers. There are many tiles available that are reminiscent of styles past: vibrantly glazed Moorish flower patterns, blue and white delf-ware, sweet peas and roses in the Arts and Crafts vein, fanciful California-style faience, and even relief styles of lotus or daisies that seem to lift right off the wall.

Computer technology is adding new realms of pattern. Photo-realistic flower images can be transferred to tiles to create one-of-a-kind mosaic walls as kaleidoscopic or refined as you like. The same technology produces unique wallpapers, too. Whether you choose hand-painted and custom-designed tiles for a wall, floral patterns for a tiled floor, or a border of blossoms for around the sink, there is sure to be exactly the right ceramic bouquet for your taste.

opposite top Just a few touches, like a rose-colored cushion and softly drooping tulips, give a utilitarian, stainless-steel kitchen warmth and friendliness. Where a wash of light would bounce off the highly reflective surfaces, small spotlights can be positioned to illuminate work areas as well as blooms.

opposite bottom left You'll want to eat more salads just so you can use these whimsical plates—complete with painted bugs.

opposite bottom right Set your table with a garden. It's a shame you have to cover these pretty plates with food!

Fresh Ways to Add Painted Blooms to Your Rooms

There are nearly as many ways to add painted and printed blossoms to a room as there are flowers in nature. Look for ideas for motifs in decorating and art books, old wallpapers, or the assortment of stencils and copyright-free images available in crafts books. Here are a few ideas to get you started—you'll find others throughout this book.

- Decoupage a serving tray with antique seed packets.
- Repaint hard vinyl flooring and stencil a floral border or stamp with flower motifs. Check craft books and websites for instructions on sanding and preparing vinyl and sealing it after it's painted.
- Stamp daisies in dark stain on a light wood floor. Make a simple daisy stamp with six corks glued together.
- Stencil flowers on plain tiles in a bathroom or kitchen. They'll need to be primed first and sealed afterward.
- Print flower and foliage designs with foam stamps to use as wallpaper or borders around windows or doors.
- Paint and sew pre-primed artist's canvas for one-of-a-kind chair cushions in the kitchen, dining room, or outdoor garden room.
- Paint a *tromp l'oeil* "rug" on a flagstone floor.
- Create a truly unique rug that's easy to clean (just mop) by painting a floor-cloth. Trim a piece of pre-primed, heavy artist's canvas to the desired size, leaving a 1" to 4" border (3.54 to 14.16 cm) for finishing on all sides, depending on the size of the rug. Draw your flowers freehand or stamp or stencil them with acrylic paints. Or use an art projector to enlarge Victorian, Art Deco, or any other floral pattern you can find and then trace the projection onto your canvas with a pencil before painting. Not handy with a paintbrush? Decoupage the rug with glued flower images cut from wallpaper or gift wrap, or iron fabric flowers onto the canvas with fusible webbing. Miter the corners for neatly finished edges. Coat the finished rug with three layers of polyurethane.

above Why decorate everything but the kitchen sink? These subtle, embossed bouquets are understated and elegant.

above *Personalize plain white cabinets with foliage of your own design or decoupage images that you scan and print yourself.*

Blooming Kitchens 61

Kitchens and Gardens Have Always Gone Together

Those lucky individuals with gardens of flowers outside their kitchen doors have no trouble bringing flowers into the kitchen by the armload. The rest of us need to use a bit more imagination to accessorize this room with blooms. There are many kitchen ideas to be gleaned from gardens, for these two spaces have a long history of compatibility.

You don't have to wrestle with a decades-old stove in order to enjoy the bucolic comfort of a vintage kitchen. Microwaves and food processors nestle comfortably with more rustic elements of wood, pottery, and fabric when united with a floral theme. With flowers, even a city kitchen can look like a garden. Give vernacular furniture a chic edge by combining natural wood with updated objects and fabrics. Find new uses for floral tablecloths from earlier decades by remaking them into shades for windows or lamps, or into placemats and napkins. Fix two or three glass shelves in front of a window and let potted flowers be your curtains. Attach a weathered iron gate or wooden trellis to the wall or ceiling to hang pots and pans. Add a skylight and feel like you're cooking in a conservatory.

above *This rustic sideboard would be equally happy in a kitchen or a potting shed. With plenty of space to work as well as store large crockery and show off floral pottery, it's functional as well as beautiful.*

below *Gorgeous Arts and Crafts style tiles with floral themes are still being made, like these from Motawi Tileworks.*

Blooming Foods

EDIBLE FLOWERS ARE PRETTY AND DELICIOUS

Flowers in the centerpiece—and in the casserole? Many of the blooms that brighten, scent, and enliven rooms can do the same for food when used as garnishes or flavorings. Cooking with flowers isn't new. Lilies, roses, violets, lavender, and many other blossoms have long been eaten in China, India, Greece, and Turkey (the Persians even tried sautéed tulip bulbs). Europeans from the Middle Ages through Victorian times devised hundreds of flower-laden recipes, including stewed primroses and carnation-petal liqueur. Nasturtiums and squash blossoms have long been common additions to native diets in the Americas. Many rural oenophiles enjoy dandelion wine, and the greens are a familiar and nutritious side dish in the South.

Before you eat any flowers, keep these pointers in mind:

- Research edible flowers. Not all flowers are edible, and some are poisonous.
- Eat only organically grown flowers (free of pesticides and chemicals).
- Pick just-opened flowers early in the day, rinse them well, and gently pat off excess water with paper towels. Check for insects and brown spots.
- Eat only the petals (in most cases), trimmed of the bitter white bases.
- Eat flowers in small amounts. Some can cause allergic reactions.
- Use only edible flowers for garnishes, even if you don't intend to eat them.
- Remember, if you can eat a plant's fruit, you can probably eat its flower, such as pea, squash, apple, or lemon.

Start your floral culinary exploration simply by eating the blooms of herbs used all the time, like rosemary, basil, or fennel. As you gain confidence, try sprinkling cornflowers or dianthus in soup, tossing nasturtiums or violets in salad, adding mustard flowers to casseroles, substituting yellow calendula flowers for pricey saffron, mixing a few elderflowers or dandelion buds into pancake batter, or stirring marigolds into stew. Add one teaspoon of dried flower petals to a cup of tea. Layer lavender or rose petals in a jar of granulated sugar. After a few weeks you'll have subtly flavored sweetener for frosting.

Try a fragrant spread for a special dinner or brunch:

Soften one stick of unsalted butter

Beat in ½ cup (118 ml) finely chopped flower petals

Season with salt, pepper, and lemon juice

Refrigerate until ready to use

You don't have to eat the flowers to enjoy them with food. They make pretty garnishes, too. Sprinkle pansies over a cake. A big hibiscus blossom (pistil and stamens removed) glamorizes a bowl of dip. Freeze whole small, edible flowers into an ice ring or cubes for punch bowls, or make a frozen bucket with embedded flowers to hold wine bottles for an outdoor party. Don't wait for a wedding to decorate a cake with crystallized violets, which can be eaten, or with other purely decorative flowers.

If allergies prevent you from eating the real thing (or the kids are too finicky), you can still serve up a bouquet of treats. Muffin tins and cake pans come in daisy and other shapes. Cut cookie dough with flower-shaped cutters and slide Popsicle sticks into the dough before baking. Decorate the cookie blooms with colored candies and sugars. Or turn vegetables and other foods into edible "flowers" with some creative slicing and arranging, like carved radish roses, chive or scallion stems, broccoli or cauliflower florets, or "petals" from olive halves, lemon peel, almond slices, or carrot shavings. Or use a knife or small, flower-shaped canapé cutters on beets or potatoes.

Blooming Kitchens

Flowers through History

Byzantine and Celtic Cultures Developed Complex Floral Motifs

In the first millennium, Byzantine artisans reshaped Greek, Roman, and Asian floral forms to achieve a distinctive formal and symmetrical style brimming with rich color and complicated designs. These they applied to silk hangings, marble inlay, frescoes, and mosaics. Realism was subdued in favor of symbolic and religious themes, but the images still included flowers, as in the "gardens of heaven" depicted in the apse of Saint Apollinare in Classe in Ravenna, Italy.

Celtic artisans adapted the Mediterranean lotus and palmette borders into their own unique curvilinear designs. The artistry of their interlocking knot and spiral designs, which culminated in the 7th century, was revitalized hundreds of years later in the Arts and Crafts movement.

Rosettes and Rich Patterns Characterized Florals of the Middle Ages

In the Middle Ages, feathery and fantastical daisies, roses, buttercups, and heartsease embellished stained glass and tile. Simple repeated patterns, called diapers, often featured fleur-de-lis or other small flowers, as did the inlaid patterns of encaustic tiles. Rosettes derived from Egyptian and Greek precursors appeared on everything from architecture to glass, metalwork, and pottery. Hand-painted flowers adorned whitewashed or plastered medieval walls, while dried blossoms decorated the rafters and scented the room. Flowers dotted the yards of tapestries and embroidered-wool wall and bed hangings that kept out drafts as well as dressed up dark or drab rooms.

above *Page of Byzantine mosaic designs from* Grammar of Ornament *by Owen Jones.*

opposite *A lady and a unicorn reside in a garden of flowers in this 15th-century tapestry called "Touch," one in a series depicting the five senses.*

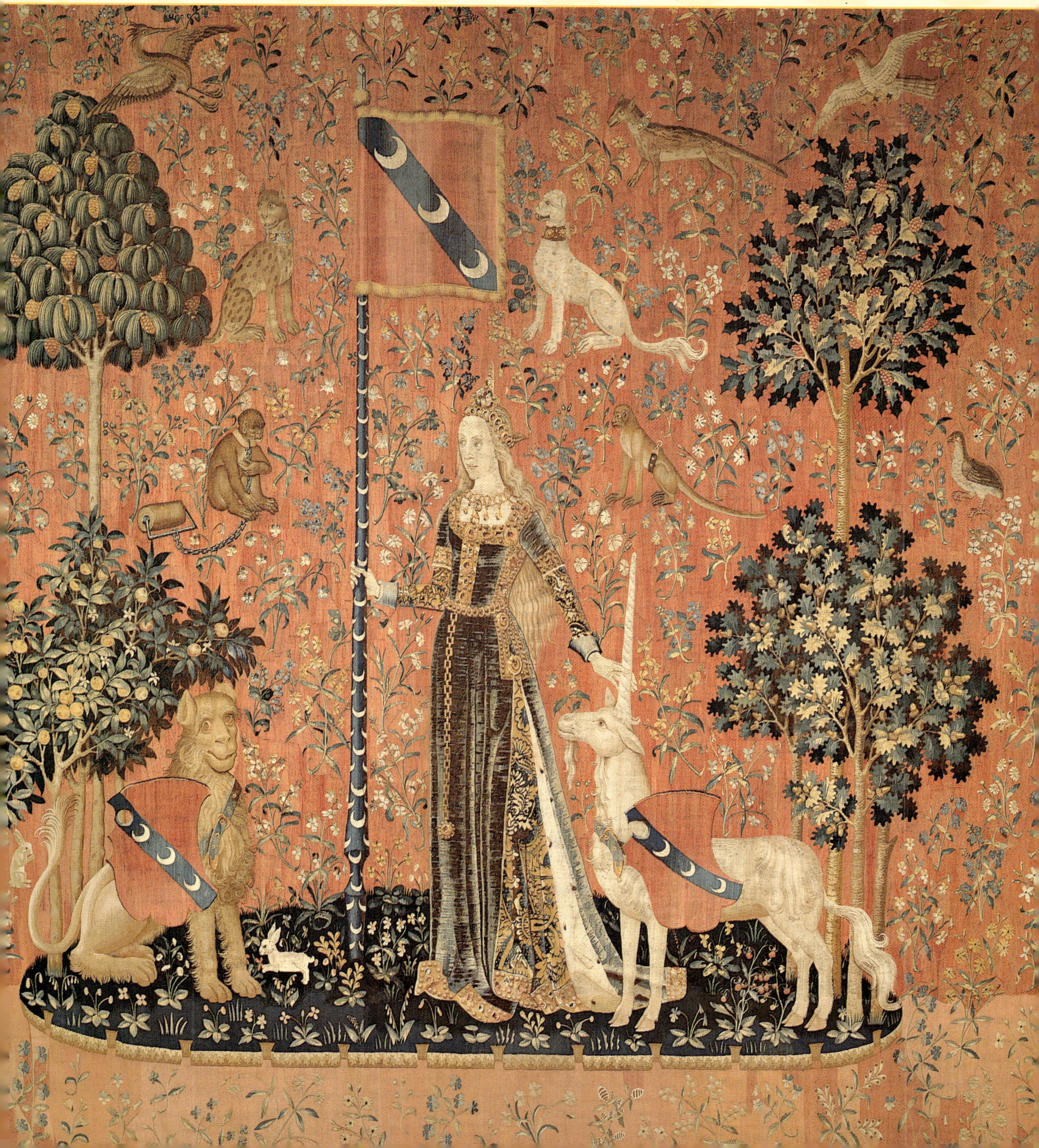

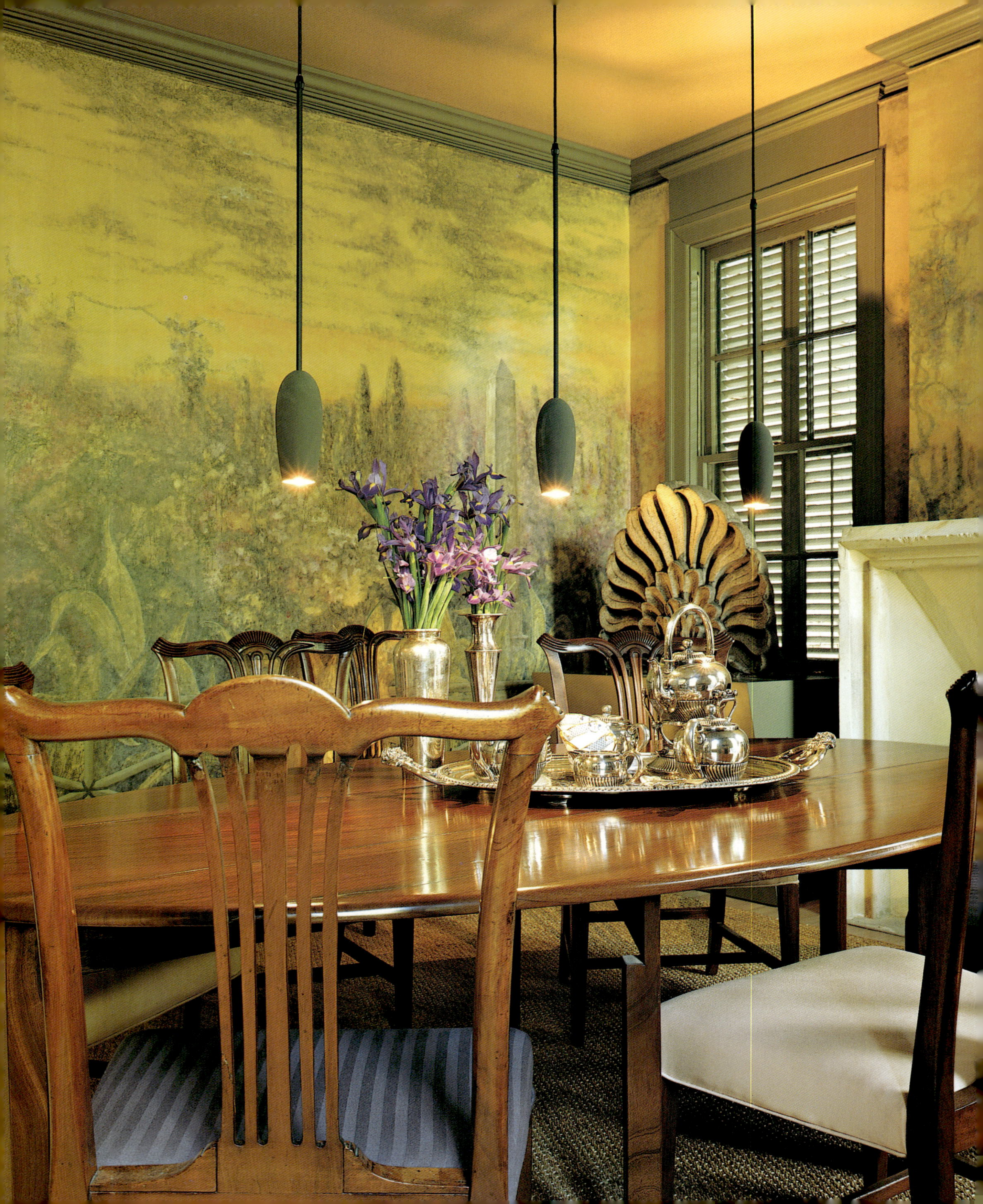

Blooming Dining Rooms

*Every flower about a house certifies to
the refinement of somebody.*

— Robert G. Ingersoll

Dining rooms have changed. In centuries past, eating at home meant taking a meal in any room in which one set up a table. Only within the last 200 years has it been common to designate a room only for dining. As a formal space reserved for Sunday dinners and special occasions, it meant using linen tablecloths, candelabras, china, stemware, and the best serving pieces. Twenty-first-century life demands a space that can sometimes do double—or triple—duty. The trend toward melding traditionally separate kitchen, dining, and living areas encourages conversation, conviviality, and communal food preparation, but the dining room hasn't lost its distinction as the one room that can dress differently for every occasion.

Few motifs surpass flowers for color, variety, and versatility, and fewer still can be considered as perfect for a dining room. Whether stripped to bare simplicity or piled in profusion, as long as you stick to a theme, color palette, or motif, you can't go wrong with flowers—no one has ever called a garden "mismatched." Be inspired by floral tradition, but add your own touches to lift your dining room out of the predictable.

opposite *Sometimes the scenery takes center stage. Even in a high-rise apartment you can eat in a garden, like this lush tromp l'oeil masterpiece. Unobtrusive ceiling fixtures keep the spotlight on jewel-toned irises or whatever centerpiece you choose as your star.*

Perform Floral Artistry and Set the Stage for Elegant Meals

More than any other room, except perhaps the bedroom, the dining room demands "atmosphere." Think of it as a stage, and use flowers, lighting, fabrics, and furniture to dress it for each performance. Like an empty stage, it's beautiful, but anticipatory. Only when the cast arrives—your guests—does the room truly come into its own. With the right accessories, it can change with the seasons or adapt for a one-act luncheon or a five-act dinner party. The dining room is accustomed to silk, crystal, and candlelight; it can stand up to a little drama, too.

A mural can make a small room seem larger. The backdrop can be a grand, realistic, or imaginative garden of paint or wallpaper. If you're hesitant to commit a whole wall, try decorating a folding screen with beautiful floral fabric or decoupage, something different on each side for quick scene changes. Or frame a tapestry or panel of antique floral wallpaper for one wall. Leaded glass screens or panels in front of windows help protect furniture and fabrics from sunlight and add a diffuse glow to the room. Prop lush floral paintings in the windows to disguise uninspiring views. Carved and distressed rosettes, palmettes, and other pieces of salvaged architecture add an air of decaying grandeur.

Theater needs the right lighting. Stage sets and makeup are all designed to work compatibly with light's colors and

above Don't wait for a special occasion to use a French tulip bowl and matching servers. Costume the table in silk and flowers and enjoy.

below Strew flowers at your guests' feet with a stunning 20th-century French Aubusson carpet that's almost too pretty to tread upon.

✿ ✿ ✿ ✿ ✿ ✿ ✿ ✿ ✿ ✿ ✿ ✿ ✿

intensity. Use lighting to accentuate your room's best features and disguise the rest. The dining room will sparkle with candlelight, of course, but also consider up-lights, down-lights, colorwashed walls, or lamps positioned to cast interesting shadows of bouquets or floral carvings. Use the soft glimmer from a candle chandelier and wall sconces to highlight repoussé blossoms on silverware, gleaming woodwork, or the shimmering flowered figures on brocade.

Rich, dark color doesn't have to mean lugubrious. Deep red is a wonderful color for a dining room, not only because complexions look rosier by candlelight, a fact any guest can appreciate, but also because every flower color looks stunning against it. Explore the theatricality of flame freesia or sophisticated deep Persian violet. Gather a troupe of colored glass vases complete with matching blossoms. And don't neglect green, from moss to forest to lily pad. Green sets off the color of virtually every flower on

above: Drama comes from pure, deep color, like dark cornflower or rich carmine walls and fabrics. The contrasting blooms, warm woodwork, and subtle floral motifs come alive against the dark backdrop.

Blooming Dining Rooms 69

earth—you can hardly go wrong using it in your "blooming" dining room.

Famed decorator Billy Baldwin once said that a room full of chair and table legs looks "restless." Pamper your guests with comfy upholstered banquettes, or cover plain wooden chairs with pleated, buttoned, or softly draped slipcovers in flowered chintz or damask. Look for vintage floral linens, tea towels, tablecloths, or blankets that can take on a new life as slipcovers. Try bleaching or tea dyeing bright new fabrics for an aged patina.

Swathe the dining table in layers, with scallop-edged linen atop a skirt of taffeta atop a flower-figured silk. Improvise with accessories—hang an Oriental tapestry on the wall or toss a paisley shawl across the table. Loosely encircle each dinner plate with long-lasting, fresh buds. Augment the table's costumes with runners of floral lace, tapestry, or beaded floral scarves. Cut flower appliqués from remnants and add them to the edge of a tablecloth. Layer the windows with sheer embroidered organdy "petticoats" beneath drapes. Add a showy centerpiece of dahlias, hydrangeas, or snapdragons, and your room is fit for a leading lady.

❀ ❀ ❀ ❀ ❀ ❀ ❀ ❀ ❀ ❀ ❀ ❀

above *Play with lighting to capture the mood and style of the event. Try covering a lackluster fixture with overlapping silk leaves or flower petals for a diffuse glow.*

Illuminate Your Blooms for the Mood and the Look You Want

Light is like the air—it's essential to life and daily activity, but we don't think about it very much. The right lighting can dramatize a floral arrangement, highlight gilded flowers on wallpaper, and cast carvings and embossed designs in high relief. The wrong lighting can cast dinner guests in a greenish hue or make it impossible to do tasks. Light fixtures provide the perfect finishing detail to a room and can coordinate beautifully with any floral theme. Once you take care of the practicalities of safety, let your imagination go.

How will the room be used? Dim, decorative lighting in the living room won't do if your favorite reading chair resides there. And just as a floodlit garden isn't conducive to romance, a wash of bright light in a room lacks mood and intimacy. A few well-placed lights can accent the sculptural qualities of blooms as well as highlight their colors. Position pin spots on a striking blossom or let them cast interesting shadows of leaves and flowers. Use colored lights if they suit the occasion and the room.

❈ ❈

There are nearly as many types and styles of lighting fixtures and lamps as there are flowers. Whether you want freestanding, wall-mounted, ceiling, or decorative, you can find one that suits your décor perfectly. Here are a few lamps to look for:

- Reproduction or antique art glass lamps
- Paper lanterns with floral designs
- Beaded fabric tulips on wire stands
- Antique candle chandeliers with painted metal flowers and leaves
- Asian-inspired lamps like oversized flower buds on slender stems
- Glass candle lamps with silk flowers submerged in liquid paraffin and essential oil—aromatherapy as well as soft atmospheric light
- Floor lamp like a slender twig holding a flower
- Table lamp like a vase of thirty tulips, each flower containing a tiny fiberoptic light
- Lily-shaped covers for bare ceiling bulbs
- Antique French glass ceiling fixture like an upside-down bouquet

Can't find precisely what you're looking for? Give a flea market find a new purpose in light.

- Transform almost anything into a candlestick or lamp—a large shell, watering can, decorative pot, or carved finial.
- Bedeck a gnarled branch with little strings of flower lights and suspend it like chandelier.
- Start with a silver-topped light bulb as the center and craft a "wall flower" recessed light fixture.
- Fashion a candle chandelier out of wire garden fencing for use outdoors.
- Light several hand-painted market umbrellas from below with low-voltage bulbs to create a garden of softly illuminated flowers.
- Glue silk or plastic flowers to strings of fairy lights for strings of lighted flowers.

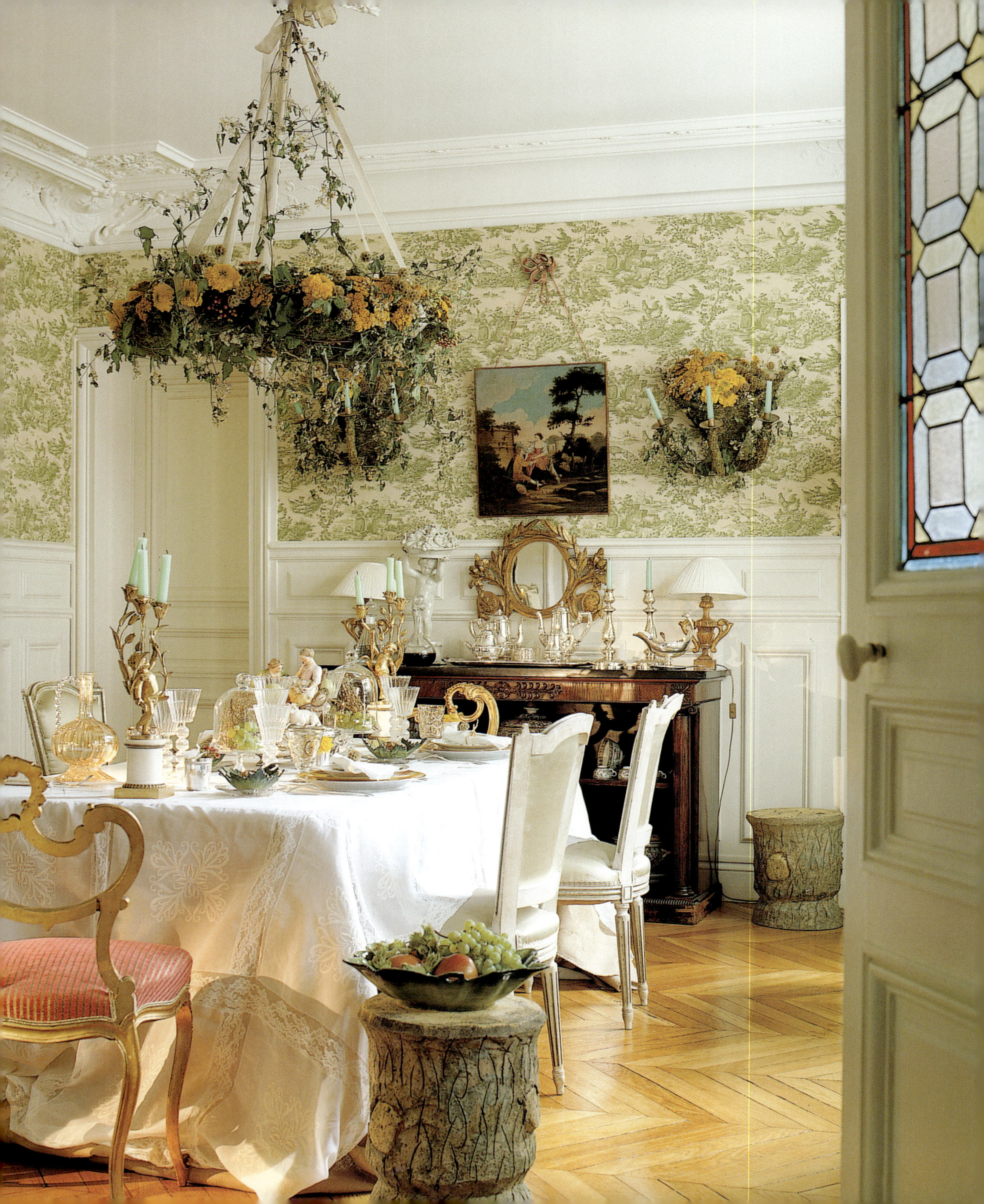

Romance a Dining Room with Lush Flowers

Romance usually conjures up crimson or pink, and who can doubt the allure of lipstick red? But don't underestimate the glamour of other palettes. Pale gray-green with cream and purply-mauve can sweep you off your feet. Indigo, teal, amethyst, and bronze all have sensual appeal and look stunning in a dining room. Deep wall color makes a room feel cozier, but you can achieve intimacy with an embrace of pattern, too. The Romans loved to paint rose-garden frescoes on their walls. Even the artistically challenged can attain beautiful effects with wallpapers, borders, paint, or art. Send flowering tree branches up to the ceiling with gilded chinoiserie wallpaper, or stencil a delicate verge of tulips. Add floral details in gilded plaster and highlight them with candlelight. Adorn a wall with a garden-themed tapestry. You can expand the room with a large wall mirror, either in an ornate carved frame or one with simple, painted flowers bordering the glass.

Vintage Victorian carpets teem with blossoms. Try an updated version of an old favorite like cabbage roses. Turning flea-market floral area rugs wrong side up mutes their tones. Dress the windows in silks, beads, lace, and delicate embroidery. Add flowers with abandon. Hang a little basket of posies from each chair or twine fresh or silk garlands across the chair backs. Look for the sensuous curves and natural motifs of the 18th-century Rococo style or Art Nouveau irises to get the room in the mood.

Drape a sparkling crystal chandelier with garlands, or find a candle chandelier decked with painted metal blossoms or bud vases. If you can't find a floral light fixture of wrought iron, brass, or porcelain, suspend a bare tracery branch from the ceiling and string it with tiny lights like white snowdrops. Disguise a ceiling fixture with a flowered Japanese parasol and mount a bouquet of pretty fans on the wall. Circle the ceiling around a fixture with ornamental plasterwork garlands or a stenciled floral wreath. Dress candlesticks with fresh or dried flower wreaths.

above *Tall centerpieces work if they're slender enough to let guests see each other and converse.*

opposite *From the putti, delicate plasterwork, toile de Jouy wallpaper, and floral "chandelier" to the carved woodwork, gilt-trimmed glassware, and layers of embroidered tablecloths, everything about this dining space spells romance.*

Scatter dried, pressed flowers across the table and smooth a layer of sheer organza or tulle over the top. Candles with pressed violets embedded in the wax softly glow with their colorful silhouettes. For a simple version, photocopy flower images onto vellum and wrap this around pillar candles. Fold napkins into pretty flower shapes or tuck a fresh bud into a pocket folded in each linen napkin. Even the condiments can dress up when placed in a small basket adorned with violets and forget-me-nots. Etching cream and floral stencils or stickers can add subtle interest to glassware.

above top *Embellish an affaire de coeur with delicately gilded or etched glassware and pastel floral china.*

above bottom *Botanical print fabrics, like these "Allium" wall hangings by artist Amanda Ross, enliven a dining room.*

Fresh Floral Arrangements Add Fragrance, Color, and Style to Every Room

The Chinese developed strict guidelines about flower type, number, and color in an arrangement. Even without rules, you can hardly go wrong when the materials are so naturally beautiful. A few simple guidelines and a bit of imagination will help you add just the right floral touch to any room.

SIZE AND LOCATION

Suit the arrangement's height, depth, and width to its setting. A bud vase won't make much of a statement in an entryway, nor will a wall of gladioli encourage conversation at dinner. Will the display be seen from all sides or just one?

FORM

- Build arrangements that are round, oval, triangular, *S*-curved, spiral, crescent, domed, square, or free-form.
- Balance the shape (note that "balance" doesn't have to mean "symmetrical"). Consider the shape of each flower, how it contributes to the look of the whole.
- Suit the space around each flower to the arrangement, such as a single bloom floating in a bowl or a dozen irises packed into a tall cylinder.

COLOR AND TEXTURE

- Season, occasion, and room decoration influence color choice. Contrast with a room color or highlight one; juxtapose contrasting colors like purple and yellow; blend related ones like blue, blue-green, and yellow; or use all one color and include shades from deep to pale.
- Texture and character come from extras like foliage, pinecones and needles, twigs, seed pods, wheat stalks, or fruits and vegetables.

CONTAINERS

Assorted containers in a variety of shapes, colors, and materials give you options. Ideas can germinate from the container as often as from the flowers. Here are some ideas for temporary, whimsical, and unexpected containers:

- Food, like pumpkins, gourds, watermelons, green peppers, or emptied eggshells
- Unusual, like seashells or driftwood
- Metal, from vintage sand pails and lunch boxes to food cans, teakettles, umbrella stands, loving cups, champagne buckets, or brightly colored 1960s aluminum tumblers
- Multiples, like eggcups, sake cups, mismatched teacups, colored glass bottles, thimbles, wine goblets, cordial glasses, ashtrays, or dessert bowls
- Plastic, such as vases, cups, even toys
- Wood and wicker, lined with a waterproof container
- Would-be castoffs, like a pottery jar, cut-glass compote, or china soup tureen missing its lid

right *A little ingenuity transforms gorgeous blooms and cranberries into a sumptuously romantic centerpiece. For monochromatic arrangements, use a range of one color. Texture comes from the varied blossom shapes, and contrast from the hints of green.*

left *Take your color scheme from Gerbera daisies, variegated roses, and a Mediterranean sky. Toss a simple length of beaded sunflower cotton over a painted table, add a modern interpretation of the floral area rug, and the result is a room that stimulates the appetite.*

opposite *Sunflowers don't have to tower overhead on leggy stalks. Try a different perspective with shallow bowls and leafy accents and let their cheerful brown and yellow faces shine.*

Bright Color and Updated Ethnic Flowers Warm Up Any Dining Experience

Vivid hues, rich bold patterns, and brilliant flowers can be found in the age-old embellishments of many cultures. Combine smart updates of these traditional floral motifs in everything from carpets to candlesticks.

Cover a table with a Mayan shawl, painted floor-cloth, paisley bedsheet, or beaded sari fabric. Deep midnight blue is just the foil for accents of violet, fuchsia, and goldenrod. Layer gold netting over a rich purple tablecloth, or silver organza over deep turquoise. Form a loose line of small pumpkins filled with daisies or arrange a clay soup tureen and a colorful explosion of Gerbera daisies. Paint removable flowers on dazzling, colored glassware using latex paint and add faux cabochons of ruby and emerald for a glittering, exotic effect. Don't be afraid to mix patterns and cultures—handcrafted Mexican chairs with deeply incised and painted calla lilies or cactus flowers, Moroccan ceramics, a Mediterranean-style sideboard, and Spanish-inspired fabrics. Complete the look with a modern version of a Turkish oushak felt rug with orange and red stylized flowers on a bittersweet chocolate ground. The elements don't have to match; they just have to look as if they've dwelled together for centuries.

Or try toned-down Mexican with whitewashed wood, adobe walls, jute floor coverings, and wrought iron fixtures—all the better for resplendent blossoms to shine. Set the table like a flower arrangement with Fiesta or Bauer ware in pure color, or use a pattern like Villeroy & Boch's "Acapulco" with its festive borders of stylized blooms and birds. Glue bright felt flower appliqués onto napkins or a tablecloth. Add napkin rings of punched or embossed copper tooling foil. Tie utensils together with raffia and squash blossoms and lay them across each plate. Finish the table with a clay soup tureen filled with hot pink cosmos. Gild the tips of a few leaves and petals in the centerpiece for a soft sheen.

Place Settings Blossom with Floral Decoration in Any Style

When it comes to china and flatware, there is a floral pattern for every taste—and then some. Look to past eras for ideas, like the Renaissance majolica pottery called *quartieri*, which featured pie-shaped sections with a unique bouquet painted in each section. Among more recent patterns, each piece of Portmeirion's "Botanic Garden" stars one of 50 different flowers, making the completed table look like a garden. If you're lucky enough to have a family set of china in a beautiful floral pattern, don't let it languish unseen in cabinets or boxes. Let it become the foundation for an assemblage of pieces that complement its color or flower. The choices in newer china couldn't be broader, from fanciful "Magic Garden" by Lenox to delicate and traditional Haviland, from Noritake's bold "Up-sa-Daisy" to vintage Minton florals, or from folk-art "Provincial" by Johnson Brothers to the subdued blue-gray of Castleton's "Gloria." No matter what your favorite flower—violet, cowslip, buttercup, or azalea—you can find it for your table.

Flowers through History

Persian Decorative Arts Bloomed with Flowers

Persian decorative art made every conceivable use of flowers, reaching its apogee in the 16th and 17th centuries. High-quality printed and painted cottons flaunted a riot of botanical shapes, from large radiating pinks to honeysuckle, poppies, and daisies on twisting stalks intertwined with flowerets of every sort. The repeated, small teardrop shapes called *boteh*, Persian for "bouquet of flowers," developed into an astonishing variety of tiny floral patterns on fabrics and eventually became what we know as paisley. Wall paintings of vases overflowed with images of fresh-cut flowers. Bright blooms adorned embroidery, ceramics, architecture, and carpets. Turkey's artistic love affair with the tulip, called *lale*, planted it on everything from earthenware to fabric. The years 1703 to 1730 are known as the "Tulip Era" in Turkey, so great was that country's obsession. Tulips were carved into buildings, tombs, and fountains and painted onto murals, pottery, and tiles. Even the guests at the sultan's lavish parties wore clothing that matched the tulips in his gardens.

Flowers Have Always Been Inextricably Linked with Carpet Design

Other than geometric patterns, flowers have surely been the most popular motifs for floor coverings. Beginning in the 13th century, Turkish carpets bloomed with carnations and lotus blossoms. Four hundred years later, "shrub" rugs featured designs of leafy, flowering foliage. Carpets from the Caucasus depicted leaf latticework with assorted flowers and palmettes. And one popular Persian design showed a flower-filled vase in a field of tendrils or lattice.

Designers of India's *mughal* carpets preferred realistic chrysanthemums. Chinese carpets drew on tradition and symbolism for floral designs, such as lotus for purity, peonies for wealth, and narcissus for winter. In the 17th century, French Savonnerie carpets were developed to harmonize with furniture and architecture from the Baroque to Art Nouveau. They favored naturalistic floral arrangements and oversized cabbage roses. Later, Aubusson factories, famous for tapestry, drew upon Savonnerie patterns to develop their own floral carpet style.

opposite, top left *Some 19th-century garden carpets, like this Persian Kirman, circa 1890, are maplike renderings of fish-filled streams subdividing plots of trees and flowering shrubs. These carpets replicated the flowerbeds and canals seen in real Persian gardens.*

opposite, top right *French Aubusson carpets, like this one from 1880, feature exquisitely elaborate and naturalistic flowers, garlands, vases, and foliage tumbling around a central medallion.*

opposite, bottom left *The floral pattern in this Bessarabian rug, circa 1890, is more geometric and stylized than that in French or Persian carpets from the same period. Red and pink were favorite flower colors in this type of carpet.*

opposite, bottom right *The flower-filled* boteh *shapes so associated with Indian paisley are clearly defined in this Turkish Borlou carpet from the late 19th century.*

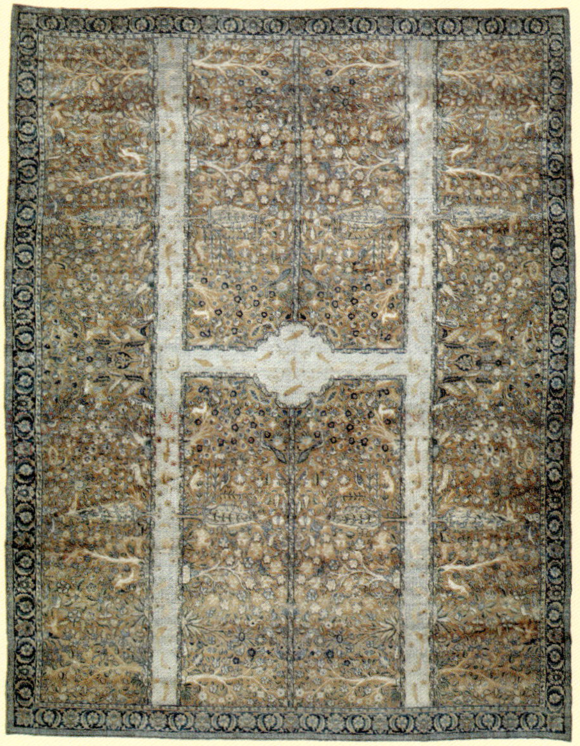
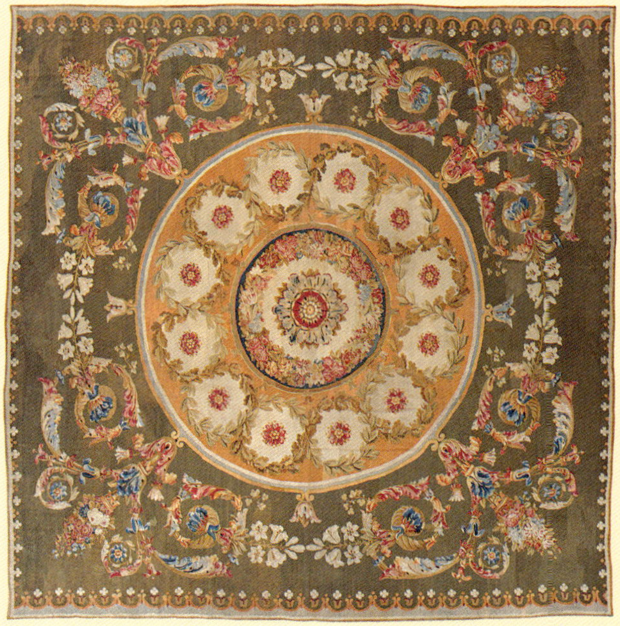
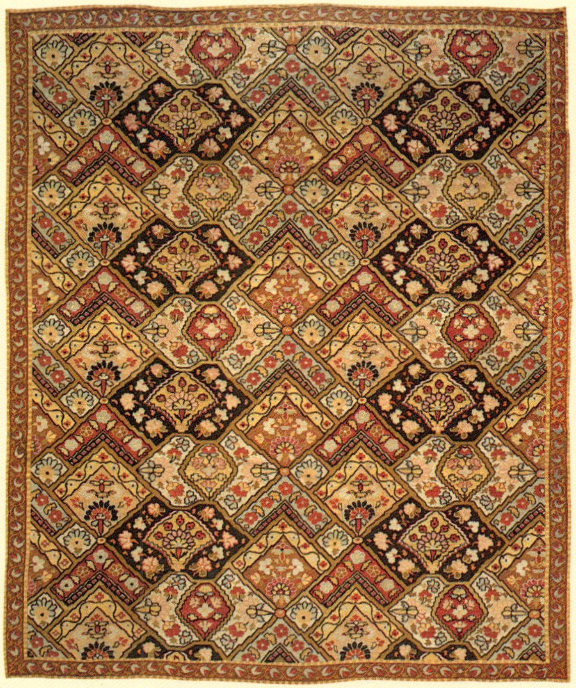
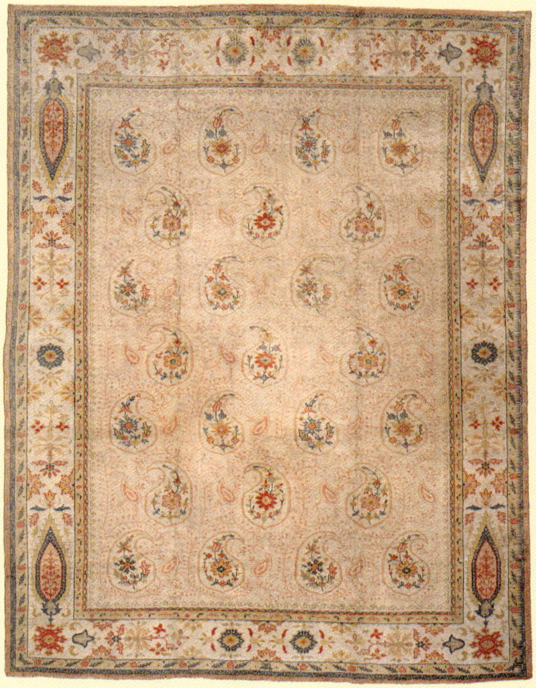

Blooming Bedrooms & Baths

The flowers that keep
Their odor to themselves all day;
But when the sunlight dies away,
Let the delicious secret out
To every breeze that roams about.

— Anonymous

The bedroom is a place for sweet dreams and secret longings—a space that supports and nourishes your most intimate self. It is a safe haven where you let down barriers and forget the world. Here you wrap in sinfully soft and sensuous fabrics to rest, relax, and replenish yourself. Blooms are not just part of the décor; their beauty speaks directly to the deepest level of your aesthetic sense. Fresh flowers create a calm, serene impact, reflecting a mood shift from a hectic day and redirecting the mind to embrace romantic energy and love. Whether your tastes lean to Japanese spare, British Raj luxury, or something between these extremes, let the flowers of a perfumed evening garden inspire you to create a room of beauty, love, and delightful dreams.

Opposite *Elegantly understated in muted and tone-on-tone colors and patterns, this bedroom invites dreamy respite from the cares of the world.*

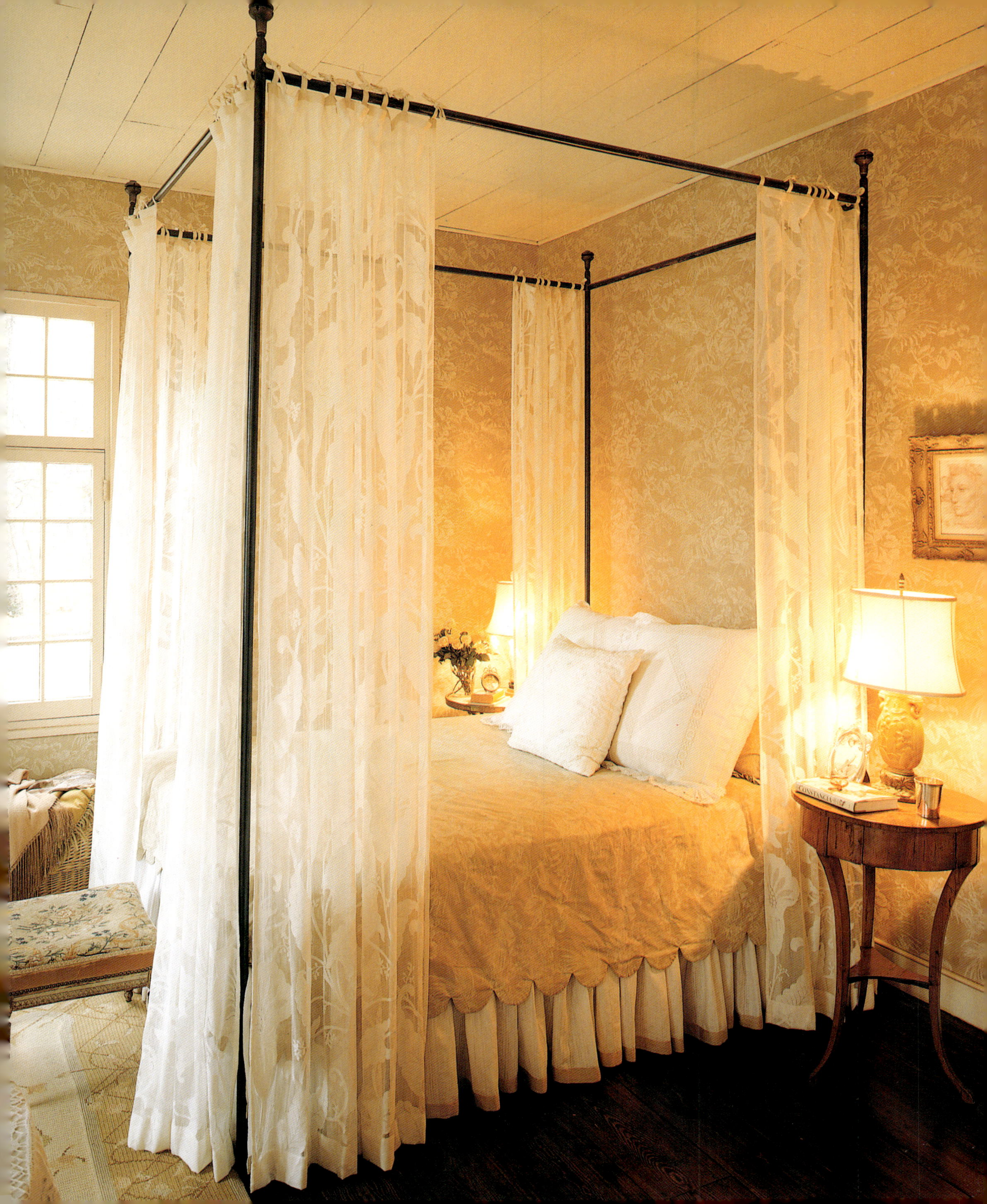

Draw Inspiration from a Moonlit White Garden

There are many types of gardens, but among those carefully planted for blooms that look best in moonlight and for their sensual perfumes, the white garden stands alone. And of all the white gardens in the world, perhaps the most beautiful is Vita Sackville-West's White Garden at Sissinghurst in Kent, England. The author envisioned her garden, planted from 1949 to 1950, as one holding white trumpet and Regale lilies, dianthus, white pansies, white peonies, white irises, and artemisia such as the lemon-scented, feathery green Artemisia abrotanum, also known as southernwood, a woody shrub that sports yellowish-white flower heads. She sought the dramatic appearance of white flowers against gray-green foliage in moonlight.

The following list includes just eight of the many flowers from purest white to palest yellow that offer both beauty and perfume to a night garden. Let these ravishing florals inspire you to grow them, paint them, and use them lavishly in your home décor.

- **Cleome**—*Cleome hasslerana*, "Helen Campbell," has white blossom balls that smell sweet from afar and are lovely in moonlight.
- **Dianthus**—*Dianthus alpinus* is the white version, with a spicy, sweet fragrance.
- **Missouri evening primroses**—*Oenothera macrocarpa* produces four-inch yellow flowers with a pleasing, sweet scent.
- **Evening stock**—*Matthiola longipetala*, four-petal, is a white flower on an 18-inch stalk with a scent compared to jasmine mixed with aromatics.
- **Madonna lily**—*Lilium candidum* has stems up to six feet that bear heavily scented, pristine white flowers.
- **Phlox**—*Phlox paniculata* has a wonderful fragrance both day and night, and butterflies love the delicate white flowers.
- **Night-blooming jessamine**—*Cestrum nocturnum*, a shrub that can reach 12 feet, blooms with creamy white, extremely fragrant flowers.
- **Tuberose**—*Polianthes tuberosa* bears creamy white, tubular flowers with a heady fragrance on stalks produced from bulblike tubers.

Sow your own white garden filled with mysterious, seductively scented plants that offer their gifts each night at dusk.

Indulge in Nights of White Satin

Create a restful, quiet bedroom interior by studying the hues, shapes, textures, and fragrances of the moonlit garden. When you are ready to begin, start by envisioning different shades of white. Consider the purest, most pristine white, soft creamy ivory, or palest lemony white, greenish white, or lilac-tinged white as a dominant color for your bed and bath. Or create a tone-on-tone effect: paint the walls a base color and use a deeper or lighter hue to create a stenciled floral pattern or stripes. Bring in accent colors—the palest blues and heavenly violets at the horizon line where sky and earth touch at twilight, the luscious silvery green of foliage in moonlight, or the softest gray of fog over a bog or misty lake just before dawn. Consider, too, reversing the color scheme with white for accents and blue, green, or gray as the base.

Let the texture of petals—silky, tissue-thin, or velvety thick—inspire you to choose luxurious fabrics for bed linens such as satin, linen, cotton, silk, and wool. Consider a white Battenburg lace bed skirt and duvet over a thick down comforter for winter and a fine matelassé coverlet embroidered in white roses or pale pansies for summer. Slip matching shams over pillows. Add accent pillows featuring flowers finely worked in bead and ribbon. Over the foot of the bed, toss a cashmere throw of mossy green, soft claret, palest peach, or muted aubergine.

Make your own creamy white bead-and-ribbon roses and attach them to a silk lampshade. Use a hot glue gun to attach fabric flowers to the top of a hatbox. Place old love letters and photographs inside. Add a little border of ribbon-and-flower wallpaper around the walls near the ceiling.

Add your favorite floral-scented oil to an unscented fabric softener sheet when drying linens. Or use lavender- or rose-scented water to dampen linens before ironing. Make beaded sachet pouches. Fill them with scented petals and herbs. Tie with ribbon and tuck them into drawers, under pillows, and in stacks of towels.

❋ ❋ ❋ ❋ ❋ ❋ ❋ ❋ ❋ ❋ ❋ ❋ ❋ ❋

opposite *Awake or asleep, you are surrounded by flowers of your dreams in bed linens and window coverings.*

right, top *Paisley, checks, polka dots, and floral patterns successfully combine for an informal country look.*

right, bottom *The curvilinear shapes of the bed and bench, along with the floral pattern of the quilt and the botanical prints, soften what would otherwise be a room of rigid angles.*

Blooming Bedrooms and Baths

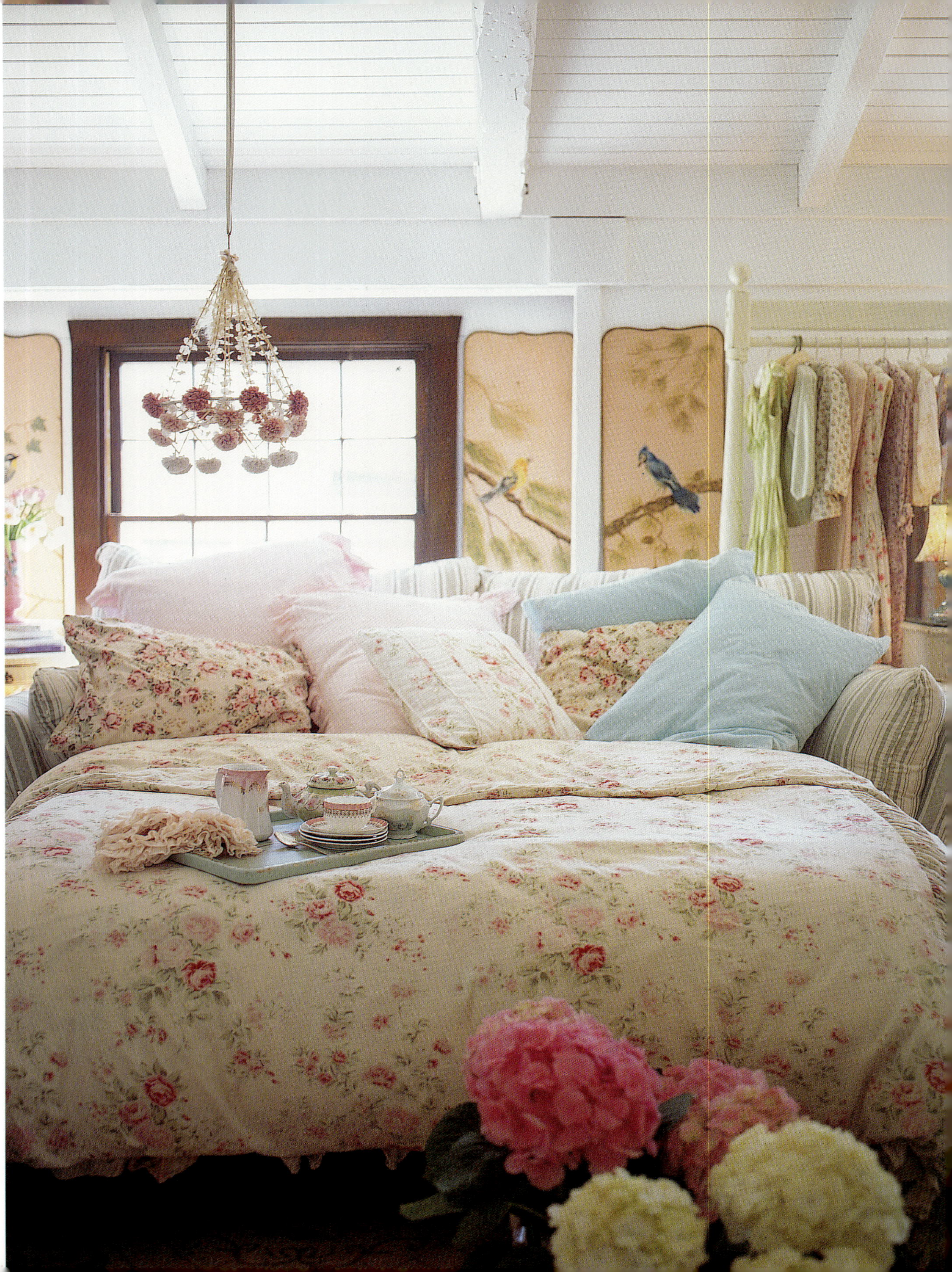

Balance the shapes in the bedroom. Observe how it is done in the garden where stems, limbs, and trunks are softened by circular, oval, or tubular-shaped flowers and foliage. If your bedroom is full of sharp lines and severe angles, add an upholstered club or wingback chair and ottoman, a canopy on a four poster bed with rounded finials, a bed bench with sloping lines, a scalloped bed skirt, or a round bedside table draped in a beautiful cloth. Find a plush rug with a floral border or one that incorporates flowers from the white garden in its design. Display it on a hardwood floor, on top of carpet, or over a bedroom banister. Hang oval-framed pictures with ribbon and flower-head tacks. Sew a fat, heart-shaped pillow and cover it with handmade silk roses, violets, carnations, peonies, or poppies. Make garlands of flowers to drape around the canopy and down each bed post. Add a cloisonné lamp with flower images on a round base. Put up a small, round mirror in a carved frame. Set out floral-shaped perfume bottles and stoppers. Decoupage floral art onto furniture and use a pen with gold ink to trace an oval "frame" around the flower.

Do you prefer a more classic, tailored style? Put in more angular and linear objects. Add a straight-back chair. Purchase or sew a chair cover made of brocade or damask (where elaborate flowers designs are woven into the silk). Add piping to accentuate angles. Hang a silk, box-pleated window topper over sheers or drapes. Set out rectangular, lined boxes or baskets to hold accessories in the bedroom and towels and toiletries in the bath. Bring in a rectangular bench for the foot of the bed. Add pictures and mirrors in square frames adorned with tiny square tiles or broken china. Stencil flowers on a wall; then enclose them in some type of square shape as part of the pattern. Use wallpaper borders to create rectangular panels on a wall, on sliding closet doors, or on a pocket door between bedroom and bath.

Refresh Body and Soul in a Blooming Bath

Are you a shower-and-go type? Then you likely prefer essential bath items to be well organized and conveniently placed. If the toilet is next to the shower, consider installing an over-the-toilet shelf unit to enable you to have everything you need within easy reach. Stack thick Egyptian cotton towels in pastel shades embroidered in white violets or gardenias. Decorate a waterproof, portable plastic caddy with those same flowers (use plastic blooms if you want to carry the caddy into the shower). In the caddy, put scented shampoo, loofah, cleansers, body wash, and conditioner. Stamp, stencil, or embroider a white flower pattern onto a pastel, lined shower curtain or sew on a captivating floral trim and hang the result. Screw a curtain tieback into the wall and twist some silk blooms around it. Glue a ceramic violet or gardenia bloom on to the backing of a plastic wall hook to hold your bathrobe. Line

above *What could be more luxurious than to soak in a warm bath filled with sensuously fragrant petals?*

opposite *Enliven a shabby chic interior with flowers in myriad forms—dried, silk, fresh, painted, and patterned on fabric.*

several baskets with fabrics patterned with these flowers. Add floral trim and fill the baskets with items such as makeup, hair dryer, styling gel, and combs. Toss a pretty throw rug embellished with flowers onto the floor. Bring in a blooming orchid to complete the look.

Love to listen to soothing strains of soft jazz while you luxuriate in a scented bath by candlelight? Your room wouldn't be complete without a fresh vase of white lilies or stalks of intensely fragrant tuberoses. Embellish your towels with ribbon embroidery or monograms. Set out a handful of soap petals (good for three to four hand washings) in the shapes, hues, and scents of flowers found in a moonlit, perfumed garden.

above *Blooming hibiscus wallpaper and curtains work their magic as a backdrop for an exquisite cabinet with its inset, scalloped basin, etched metal hardware, and ornate molding.*

Flowering Furniture
CARVED, PAINTED, OR APPLIED

Turn a simple armoire into a stunning conversation piece with painted blossoms. Paint the furniture. Let it dry. Hand paint flowers over it. Or trace blossom branches or a floral still life and transfer the image to the furniture. Paint the image onto the wood. Apply varnish or age it first using crackling medium.

Decoupage pieces of patterned paper, pictures of your favorite flowers (flower catalogs are great resources for this), gold and silver decorative paper, old letters, and prints of illustrated manuscript pages or historical documents onto small tables or chairs, mirror frames, and salvaged furniture.

❈ ❈

BLOOMING IDEAS: HOW TO DECOUPAGE A BOX OR A PIECE OF FURNITURE

- ❈ Find gorgeous floral images by searching through gardening magazines, seed catalogs, and museum and art publications.
- ❈ Choose a piece of furniture or a box to decorate. Paint and let it dry.
- ❈ Make color photocopies of the flower images and carefully cut them out, including stems and foliage. (Images from throwaway magazines or catalogs can be cut out and used directly.)
- ❈ Create a bouquet on the furniture or box. Securethe images with a dab of white craft glue or decoupage glue.
- ❈ Apply decoupage glue with a sponge brush over everything. Let dry.
- ❈ Add an element of drama—stencil a border; antique the entire piece with a wash of burnt umber, burnt sienna, or raw umber acrylic paint; or write flower names and garden verse in a gold or silver ink.
- ❈ Apply a coat of clear matte varnish. Or, if you're using Asian motifs and you want a lacquered look, paint the piece with layers of high-gloss varnish.

above *A simple leaf pattern dresses up this vanity*

Blooming Bedrooms and Baths   87

Frost a bathroom window with etching spray, or do a variation by creating a template of your favorite flower or the word *flor*, Spanish for flower, or *baño*, Spanish for bath (you could use any other language as well). Buy a waterproof, inflatable bath pillow with suction feet. Cover it with tissue-thin fabric embellished in flowers and seed pearl beads around the outside edges. Create slits or "buttonholes" so the suction feet can stick through. Use the pillow during long, sensuous soaks. For unabashed decadence, place a sliding bathtub tray over the tub to hold a flower-adorned candle, a bottle of water or glass of champagne, a chocolate truffle, and a book of garden essays.

Make your own scented bath and massage oils. Use a favorite floral or herb fragrance. Pour the oil into pretty bottles and add a decorative label and ribbon. Or create your own botanical bars of soap—add petals, essential oils, and colorant. Pour the soap mixture into molds and let it harden. Decorate the bars with gold luster wax or paint. Wrap them in beautiful paper and seal with melted wax stamped with a flower emblem. Make an eye mask out of satin and fill it with petals from a white, perfumed garden.

Use Japanese Sensibility to Style It Serene and Spare

In a Japanese garden, each stone, waterfall, stream, plant, tree, hill, path, bridge, or building serves an individual purpose, but each thing also adds to the sense, integrity, and unity of the whole. In fact, the garden's beauty is in its symmetry and simplicity. This concept works equally well when creating an uncluttered, orderly, functional, beautiful, yet spare environment in a bedroom or bath. Use the same palette of white and muted colors discussed at the beginning of this chapter to create a peaceful ambience conducive to contemplation, rest, meditation, and sleep.

Paint the room (try lavender-gray for the walls and several shades lighter for the ceiling). Move in a futon bed or set a mattress on a wooden platform over a tatami mat. Place a table along a wall to hold a piece of contemporary or antique Japanese sculpture, a bonsai plant, or a small stack of much loved books. Remove all clutter. Incorporate the ancient floral and foliage images of Japan, such as bamboo, chrysanthemums, lilies, plum blossoms, flowering cherry, and wisteria. Find these centuries-old patterns in historical fabrics and furnishings such as costumes, screens, and boxes. Make a quilt out of flower-patterned kimonos of vintage silk (crafted from the fibers produced by Japanese silkworms). Sew accent pillows with images such as the sweetly fragrant and splendidly white versions of the Japanese tree peony. Decoupage a dresser with Japanese floral designs. For a lacquered look, finish the dresser with several coats of varnish, allowing each one to dry thoroughly. Place an ikebana arrangement of fresh flowers front and center.

opposite *Flowers are beautiful in every setting, but especially so when staged amid reflective surfaces such as marble, mirror, glass, or silver.*

above *Crazy for flowers? Let it show. Spruce up a wall of a small bathroom with petals on paper and blooms in decorative pots or baskets.*

Floral-Scented Rooms
HOW TO MAKE FRAGRANT PASTILLES AND BEADS

Use scented pastilles to enhance dry potpourri. Tuck them into drawers and linen closets. Hang the beads from drawer pulls or string them on ribbon with large wooden, glass, or other decorative beads for a pretty way to scent a room. Back a string of them with wide velvet ribbon and tie back drapes. Experiment by mixing floral and woody or green scents. Let your nose decide!

These cookie-like shapes are not edible. Keep them out of the reach of small children. This recipe makes about 32" (2.5 cm) pastilles or beads.

Lavender

Ingredients

- ¼ cup (59 ml) powdered orris root (iris root) or calamus root (sweet flag) *
- 1½ tsp. essential oil (try rose, honeysuckle, or lavender; or mix a floral with bergamot, rosemary, myrrh, or frankincense)
- ¼ cup (59 ml) ground or powdered dried flower petals or dried fragrant herbs
- ½ cup (118 ml) gum tragacanth (a liquid-absorbing food additive) *
- ¾ cup (177 ml) water

* See resource guide for sources.

Instructions

1. Wearing disposable gloves, use your fingers to mix the first three ingredients in a glass, ceramic, or metal bowl. The mixture will have a wet-sand texture.
2. Add gum tragacanth and mix.
3. Add enough water to make a sticky dough. Mix it with your fingers.
4. Place the dough on a sheet of waxed paper or aluminum foil and cover with a piece of waxed paper. Roll to about ⅛" to ¼" (3 to 6 mm) thick. (Wood will absorb the scented oils. Do not reuse a wooden rolling pin for food.)
5. Cut the dough with small, flower-shaped cookie cutters to make pastilles.
6. Or roll beads between pieces of waxed paper on a smooth surface.
7. Dry the pastilles for 48 hours, turning them over occasionally.
8. Let the beads sit for an hour or two, pierce them with a skewer, and then let them dry for a day or two before stringing.

To make simpler pastilles, soak modeling clay shapes in essential oils, blot off the excess oil, and let the pieces harden in the air or in an oven set on low (follow the baking directions on the package of clay that you use). These pastilles have the advantage of being more decorative, since you can make them in bright flower colors.

Bedazzle with British Raj

When British merchants set up shop in India to bring spices and other treasures back to Britain, a highly portable type of furniture known as campaign furniture evolved to serve the needs of British officers sent to far-flung corners of the Empire. Families of British soldiers, civil servants, and merchants posted to India brought or shipped their treasured furnishings, linens, and china. For these travelers who wished to keep up appearances of respectability and class, British furniture makers created distinctly English furniture that was elegant, highly portable, and easy to set up, whether in a tent or in a bungalow.

As for flowers in their new homes, British memsahibs seemed to adore roses especially, and they made sure rose bushes were planted in gardens and in British cemeteries on the hot subcontinent. While it probably did not matter much to the gentlemen, these resilient ladies, ever English in sensibility, would have loved fresh-picked roses for their bedrooms.

Create a British Raj Look with Linen, Nottingham Lace, and Period Artifacts

Here are a few ideas to get you started. Move in a four-poster mahogany or brass bedstead. Make the bed in beautiful white linen, embroidered or trimmed in lace. Create and hang a sumptuous canopy of curtains in silk damask. Trim the curtains in tasseled fringe and rosettes. Paint a wall-mounted, peg shelf with roses. On the pegs, hang a topee, antique binoculars, and an old-fashioned camp lantern.

Bring in a mahogany dresser and cover it with a white lace dresser scarf. Set out an antique-looking, engraved, silver mirror and brush, along with black-and-white pictures of loved ones in silver frames. Reupholster a wing-back chair in faded chintz. Throw a Nottingham lace tablecloth over a carved pedestal accent table and situate the table next to the chair. Position a few books and a tea tray on the table.

Make a collage from period letters, an old locket, train tickets, a pressed corsage, and a military tea dance pass.

above Don't wait for the monsoon season to bring the garden indoors. These blooms brighten year-round.

Scavenge old magazines for images such as English garden ads, old seed catalog pictures, and flower art from the British Raj period. Decoupage these and other historical images onto boxes, furniture, or screens. Hang sepia portraits of people from that time. Scour stamp shows for vintage postcards and stationary from the Indian princely states or provinces that were governed by maharajas and nawabs. Place them on top of a large, leather steamer trunk and cover them with a heavy sheet of glass to protect them.

Carve rosettes from wood and attach them with glue to the four corners of a bookcase with grillwork doors. Install floral-engraved, brass wall sconces with chimneys and glass bulbs shaped like candles, or add a brass Victorian pole lamp with frosted glass shades. Install a ceiling fan. Hang filmy, white window curtains for a romantic feeling or install matchstick shades. On the floor, spread some dhurries embellished with the lotus flower ornamentation found throughout India.

Flowers through History

European Ornamentation Flowered in Renaissance, Baroque, and Rococo Styles

Renaissance Europe luxuriated in floral patterns tinged with wildness. Flowers bloomed along borders and on enamelware, tapestries, earthenware, and marquetry. Flowers and foliage seemed to take root in the wood, metal, or marble from which they were wrought. Embroidered silks shimmered with foliated scrolls and botanical arabesques. Italian weavers elaborated upon Indian lotus motifs and Islamic decorations to create a pattern called "pomegranate" that can still be found today. Flowers and sweet-smelling herbs were strewn on the floors of common and fine homes alike. Grander houses flaunted decorated ceilings with elaborate floral plaster swags and festoons.

The Baroque style that began in 17th-century Italy featured fantastical and profuse floral and plant decorations. The first flocked wallpaper appeared at this time. Its velvety surface, achieved by painting a design with adhesive and then applying a layer of powdered wool to the adhesive, lent itself perfectly to floral themes. The finest homes included wood paneling called *boiserie*, elaborately decorated with shallow relief carvings of flowers, foliage, swags, and urns. Or these homes might display indoor walls and ceilings that mimicked nature with realistic trellises and three-dimensional roses all carved out of plaster. Cabinetmakers crafted furniture with intricate marquetry flowers of multicolored woods, tortoiseshell, and mother-of-pearl. Popular evocations of Chinese floral motifs, particularly wallpaper, reappeared on chinoiserie throughout Europe.

The imaginative yet refined curvilinear motifs of the Rococo style were well suited to sensuous flower and plant forms in the 18th century. Floral and shell shapes curved over chairs, and sprigs of painted flowers sprouted from tableware. Expensive furniture might be inlaid with flowers of abalone, ivory, and brass. Luscious upholstery fabrics included caramel-colored moiré embroidered with honeysuckle and butterflies. Sunflower medallions, loops of flower garlands, and cherubs holding roses were carved into mantelpieces. Wall coverings and bed hangings of tapestry and damask were often richly covered with roses and other flowers. Vases of floral arrangements brightened painted chimney boards, which fit into fireplaces in the summer to keep out drafts and soot.

above *In the late 17th century, every nook was ripe for embellishment. This painted panel by Carlo Maratta was intended to fit over a door.*

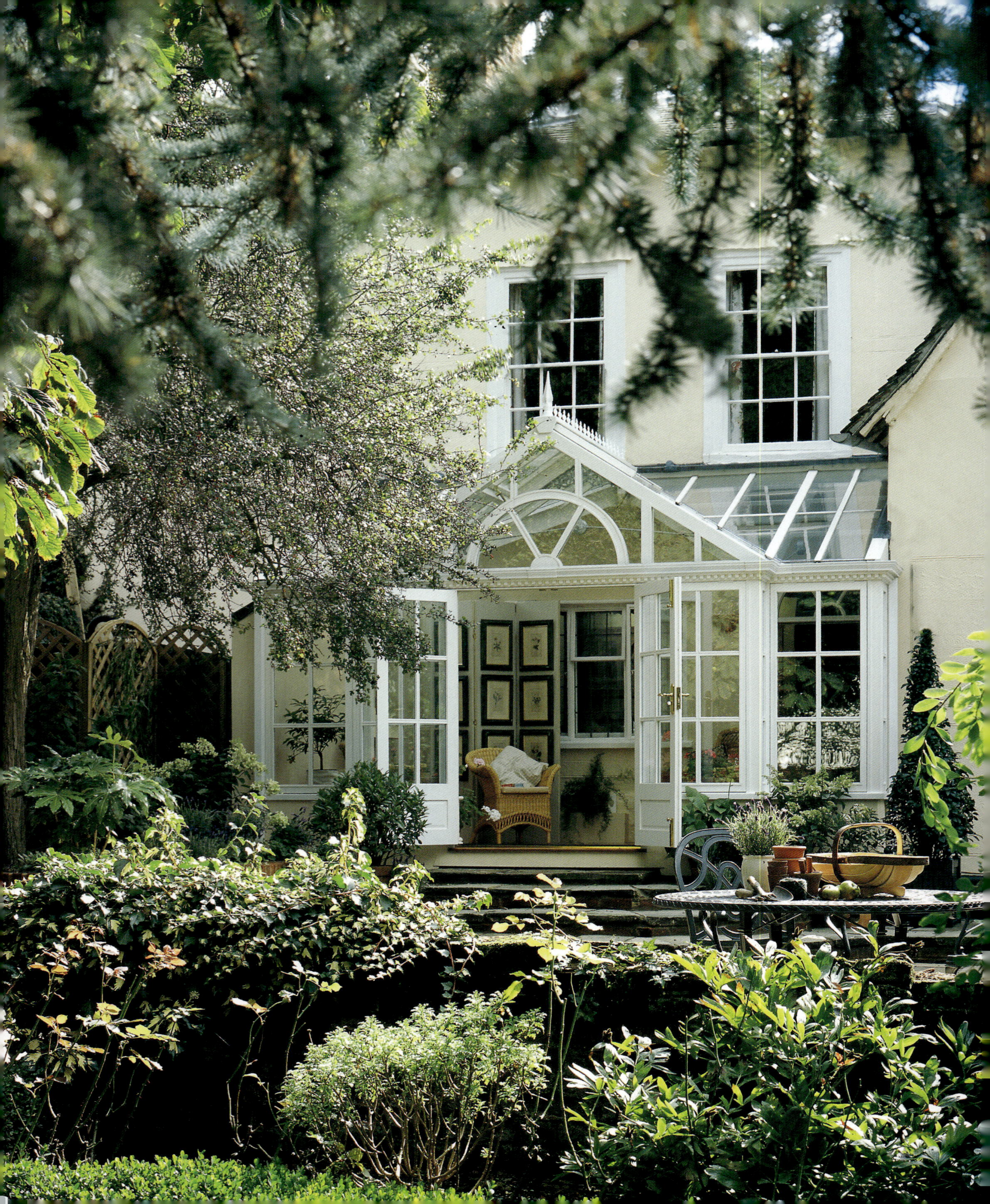

Blooming Indoor Garden Rooms

More things grow in the garden than the gardener sows.

❧ Spanish proverb

The indoor garden room has been called by many names—arboretum, conservatory, orangerie, atrium, greenhouse, and sunroom. While these names may all evoke similar images of indoor spaces with lots of glass to let in natural light and views of the outdoors, such rooms can take many forms. One might be ornate and expansive, looking as though it belonged to a European villa, while another might be attached to a wall of a simple stone cottage. How you decorate your garden room interior will depend on whether it will be used for specific tasks, for entertaining, or for simply growing plants. The process of decorating a room that nourishes you as well as the plants is both satisfying and fun.

Create a Grand Room Inspired by History and Paintings

If you have moved into a house with a conservatory or are thinking of adding one, you might be curious about the origin of such a space. During the 15th century, when wealthy Europeans wanted to protect their precious citrus trees from the inhospitable climate of northern Europe,

opposite *The yellow wicker surrounded by potted plants and the framed botanical prints on the wall give this room a classical, timeless appearance.*

they built wooden and stone structures—many of them simple constructions. When the winter weather became extremely harsh, they would heat these utilitarian shelters with small fires. Eventually, these buildings were enlarged and modified to accommodate narrow glass windows in the roof, allowing sunlight to pass through. Known as orangeries, they housed orange trees and other exotic plants brought to Europe from around the world. Later on, these orangeries were de rigueur adjuncts to the homes of the wealthy.

Orangeries became fairly common all over northern Europe. The English, who adored flowers and gardening, transformed the orangeries into greenhouses. Filled with plants during the winter months, the greenhouses served during the summer months as lovely, informal spaces for entertaining. Leave it to the Victorians and their obsession with ornamentation to transform greenhouses into elaborate and elegant confections to house their exotic botanical specimens. Today, you can visit some beautiful conservatories in Europe's stately homes, but for the average homeowner, the massive size needs to be scaled down.

Find Inspiration in Art Depicting Conservatories and Garden Rooms

To design and decorate your own conservatory in the grand European style, even if your room is small, start by viewing classic paintings of greenhouse rooms from the period you wish to recreate. For example, if you like the Victorian period, examine paintings such as *In the Greenhouse*, by Edouard Manet; *Chrysanthemums*, by Charles Courtney Curran; and *Adelaide Maria, Countess of Iveagh*, by George Elgar Hicks. Elegant conservatories and lush garden rooms inspired painters of that era. Study James Jacques Joseph Tissot's painting, *Chrysanthemums*. Flowering chrysanthemums of every imaginable shape and color dominate this painting and dwarf the kneeling model whose red hair and yellow shawl resonate with the colors of the flowers. Also examine Tissot's *The Rivals*. This painting captures the elegance and stunning beauty of a plant-filled conservatory

above *The basic lean-to style is given a modern look here, where two houses, linked by the construction, benefit from the space and the garden beyond.*

furnished in high style with lavish burgundy and blue carpets, color-coordinated drapes, blue and yellow ceramic vases and lamps, and marvelous mirrors, tables, and chairs. The men and women in the painting are sharing gossip and tea, an agreeable and common activity for the wealthy of that period.

With protected space, plenty of light, and (presumably) controls to allow you to artificially create a specific type of ecological environment, you, like the Victorians, can grow almost anything your heart desires, from medieval plants such as the Madonna lily to carnivorous plants like the Venus flytrap and everything in between. The Victorians loved exotic plants—the more unusual the better. They enjoyed everything from cacti (plants that require a dry climate like the desert) to proteas and rare orchids (which require a climate more like that of a rainforest). But they also appreciated the simple beauty of plants that are commonly cultivated today.

Use Plants the Victorians Loved

- **Anthurium**—tropical jungle plants with dark green leaves and gorgeous flower bracts in luscious reds, pinks, and whites
- **Begonia**—tuberous, rhizomatous, or fibrous-rooted plants that are often displayed in hanging baskets to dramatize the dazzling hues of their flowers and the dramatic color of leaves that range from dark green to maroon, lilac, rose, and silvery gray
- **Bougainvillea**—evergreen, shrubby vines with dazzling flower color that ranges from magenta, rose, and pink to gold, yellow, and white
- **Bottlebrush**—shrubs or small trees with dense flower brushes in crimson, pink, and yellowish-green
- **Camellia**—evergreen shrubs with colorful flowers in stunning shapes, including semi-double, formal double, and peony, anemone, and rose forms
- **Chrysanthemum**—easy-to-grow annuals and perennials valued for their dependable summer and fall color
- **Cycad**—a favorite for Victorian conservatories and generally thought of as palms, but actually a member of the Cycadales—slow-growing, evergreen plants with either palmlike or fernlike leaves
- **Dieffenbachia**—evergreen indoor plants grown for their exquisite foliage
- **Ficus**—ornamental figs with lovely foliage and bark
- **Fuchsia**—both evergreen and deciduous shrubs with an abundance of showy flowers
- **Geranium (shown)**—easy-to-grow perennials with year-round green leaves and showy flowers summer to fall in a wide variety of intense colors
- **Honeysuckle**—sweetly fragrant, evergreen, deciduous shrubs or vines
- **Hydrangea**—dramatic foliage and huge clusters of long-lasting flowers that hold their color
- **Iris**—bulbs or rhizomes that produce spiked foliage and fragrant flowers
- **Lily**—perhaps the most gorgeous of all the bulbous plants, with trumpet- or flat-shaped flowers in many lovely colors
- **Orchid**—stately flowers loved because of their exquisite, exotic, and long-lasting blooms, once so expensive that only the very wealthy could afford them
- **Passion flower**—evergreen or deciduous shrubs with profuse, showy flowers ranging from salmon and white to pink and purple
- **Protea**—evergreen shrubs native to South Africa and highly valued for their exotic flower heads, which make excellent, long-lasting cut flowers
- **Rose**—perhaps the best-loved plant in the world and one the Victorians cultivated in their gardens and greenhouses because of its attractive foliage, gorgeous blooms, colorful and medicinal hips, and luscious scents

Victorian Relationships Bloomed or Withered with the Messages Encoded in Flowers

We use flowers to commemorate and celebrate every sort of occasion. Today, we base our flower selections more on the preferences of the recipient than on any particular meaning the flower may have. The choice of flowers hasn't always been so casual.

The Greeks, Persians, Indians, and Chinese all ascribed symbolic meaning to flowers. The wife of the British ambassador to the Turkish Sultan's court, Lady Mary Wortley Montague, is credited with bringing the language of flowers to England in 1716. But it was the Victorians who grabbed the idea and turned it into a science, codifying every type of flower, leaf, grass, and herb, as well as their colors, combinations, and orientation. The meaning of a flower changed depending on where it was worn. Even the type of ribbon and the way it was tied could turn a query into a refusal. A strategically arranged nosegay expressed emotion as explicitly—if not more so, for the poetically challenged—as a handwritten note. And the message could be surreptitious, too, since only those who knew the "code" could decipher the message. If a young lady received a bouquet of jonquils and snowdrops, she knew her suitor shared her affection and had hope for a continued friendship. But should a woman return an ardent Romeo's orange roses (for passion) blossoms down, no words were necessary to tell him to buzz off.

Marigold—grief

Use the flower meanings from the list to create a bouquet, or apply them to a decorating scheme, using their colors and images in appropriate rooms of your home. For example, energize a home office with hollyhock (ambition), lemon blossom (zest), clematis (ingenuity), and hepatica (confidence)—it couldn't hurt!

- Acacia—friendship
- Amaryllis—timidity
- Azalea—temperance
- Bluebell—constancy
- Camellia, red—excellence
- Chrysanthemum, white—optimism
- Cowslip—pensiveness
- Dock—patience
- Geranium—melancholy
- Heliotrope—devotion
- Honeysuckle—affection
- Jasmine—cheerfulness
- Larkspur—fickleness
- Lily, white—sweetness
- Lotus—eloquence
- Mimosa—sensitivity
- Narcissus—conceit
- Nasturtium—patriotism
- Oleander—beware
- Pansy—thoughts
- Peony—bashfulness
- Periwinkle, white—pleasant memories
- Poppy—consolation
- Sweet Pea—departure
- Thistle—austerity
- Violet, blue—modesty

Poppy—consolation

Snapdragon—desperation

Columbine, purple—folly

Lilac—innocence

Daffodil—regard

Buttercup—childishness

Foxglove—insincerity

Blooming Indoor Garden Rooms

above *A glass cloche, old watering can, and distressed urn add textural interest and an element of intrigue to this garden room. One wonders about the personal history of each of these objects.*

above *This woodwork basket with ornamental linears at top and bottom is a reproduction of a French* boiserie, *circa 1740. This one can be used as a decorative centerpiece on a fireplace, stove hood, cornice, over-the-door panel, or mirror.*

Add Period Furnishings and Furniture in Soft Colors

Keep in mind that the dominant color of a garden room will be shades of green with splashes of vibrant color from blooms. Add accents of white, brown, straw, muted yellow, or almost any soft hue that you find pleasing. Choose durable floor materials such as decorative tile, slate, terrazzo, reclaimed brick, and stone. Wood flooring is warm and lovely, but moisture can cause it to warp or crack. Add chairs and tables of wicker, cane, bamboo, stone, or wrought iron accented with beautiful floral cushions. Hang gossamer fabrics embellished with flowers over the lower windows to create a bit of privacy as well as provide protection from the heat of the sun. Some Victorians even used heavy drapes over the windows and Oriental rugs on marble floors.

Ornate moldings, paneling, pilasters, window and cornice work, and decorative glazing bars are often characteristic of the conservatory room, so search architectural salvage shops for any of these, as well as for old carved cornices, over-door panels, friezes, and ornamental mirrors. Scavenge for chairs and tables made of cane from the rattan palm or of wood with the rush seats popular during the 18th and 19th centuries. Add a carved table, antique or reproduction, for refreshments, games, and gossip. Move in tables with marble tops to hold gorgeous vases of your colorful blooms. The Victorians elevated the process of arranging flowers in exquisite vases (sometimes in multiple tiers) to a high art.

Introduce Plant Stands, Stone Pillars, and Garden Artifacts with a History

Position plants on a decorative jardiniere or étagère or on wooden or wire plant stands. Add any artifacts that look as though they may have lived in a conservatory or garden room in another lifetime—for example, a glass cloche or a bell-shaped jar. Hang spider plants and blooming begonias from the ceiling. Arrange moisture-loving plants around a fountain. Place different varieties of shrubs and houseplants on tables and stone pillars. Arrange bushy potted plants around the perimeter of the floor. Add classical-style stone busts or statuary amid the lush layering of plants. Use tall palms, small trees, and gigantic ferns generously.

Bring seasonal color to any drab areas by moving in moss-encrusted urns and old pots of blooming perennials, bulb plants, and orchids. Hang glass wall vases and fill each one with a stunning single blossom. Place large masses of flowers—one type, one color, for the most dramatic impact—in glittery cut glass or crystal vases.

Buy or make wind chimes of sparkling beads, ceramic flowers, broken pieces of old china, old keys, and jewelry; hang them in a breezy passageway. Add an antique birdcage and fill it with fresh rosebuds embedded in wet floral foam that's encircled with a cardboard collar and covered in lace. Embellish small, pastel-colored pots with silk ribbon, plant them with miniature roses, and group them around the room. Add a curule stool with a rose damask-covered seat. On a wire hat stand, toss a wide-brimmed straw hat with a ribbon band and massive silk or velvet flowers.

Lighting for gray days and evenings has to be considered even in a room made mostly of glass. Choose reproduction or antique Victorian gasoliers or pole and table lamps with reproduction Victorian shades hand-painted with flowers, or use shades sewn in a rich-looking fabric and trimmed in silk ribbon, beads, or feathers. Don't worry about getting too ornate—as far as the Victorians were concerned, that was impossible.

Go Tropical with a Retro Hawaiian Room

You may not have a garden room that faces onto a palm-fringed beach with the islands of Molokai and Lanai towering in the distance, but by creating your own retro Hawaiian-style room, you can still step back into the 1950s. Revisit a time when a "woody" carried surfboards to the beach and tropical life moved at an unhurried pace with no intrusive cell phones and laptops. In this room, you can enjoy the scents of tropical flowers while you sip a mai tai and replay in your mind images from movies such as *South Pacific* and *From Here to Eternity*. If you prefer parrots and hot Caribbean colors, follow your passion. The same general principles of decorating in a tropical style apply.

Start with Beautiful Plants Grown in Paradise

Use flowering vines with gorgeous color such as bougainvillea, morning glory, glory bush, cup of gold, and passionflower against trellises or wall supports for a jungle-style garden. Add the graceful elegance and heavily perfumed plants of the ginger family, including blue, shell, red, and yellow kahili ginger. In woven baskets, insert pots of native Hawaiian white hibiscus (which can grow to 30 feet, or 9.1 meters), the slightly smaller, red Chinese hibiscus, ti plants (considered good luck), and, of course, anthurium (which is so perfect in appearance that frequently people don't believe it is a living plant). Finally, bring in blooming orchids for their graceful foliage, long flower stems, and exquisite blooms in myriad colors. Choose from these Hawaiian favorites: dendrobium, phalaenopsis or moth orchids, vanda, and cattileya orchids.

❋ ❋ ❋ ❋ ❋ ❋ ❋ ❋ ❋ ❋ ❋ ❋ ❋

opposite *The lampshade's colors and fringe, the floral wall painting, and the parrot and ceramics work nicely together to create a tropical feeling.*

left *Move in a sofa with an ethnic print, add a palm tree, display pieces of folk art, and enjoy instant tropical ambience.*

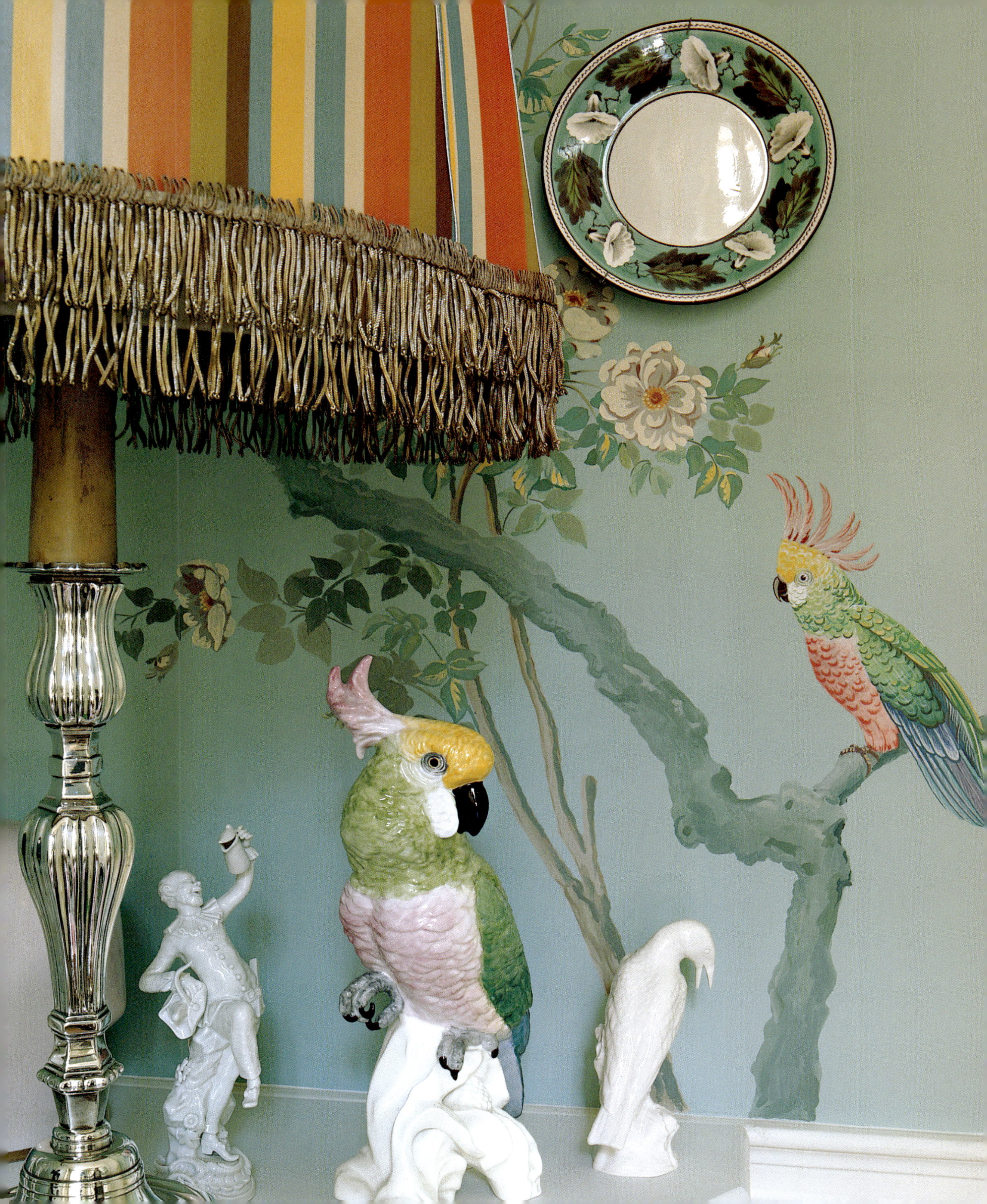

How to Choose the Best Containers for Fresh Flower Displays

* **Pick a focal point.** Blooms? Foliage and branches? Stems? If you answered yes to the last, pick a cylindrical, transparent vase that lets you see the stems. Tie the stems of a bunch of tulips, callas, lilies, or daffodils with pretty ribbon in two or three increments up the stems, or braid the stems with ribbon before placing them in a snug-fitting glass container with water.

* **Choose the right height.** Fat, squat vases fit the small flower heads of hydrangea, but tall bud vases suit long-stem roses. Shallow bowls and saucers are ideal for single blooms of camellias, dinner-plate-size dahlias, larger Gerbera daisies, or water lilies. A large Chinese pot on a pedestal is perfect for potted plants. Small pots can be used for large, massed blooms or dramatic arrangements. Use small, wall-mounted bud vases for a solitary spot of color.

* **Study the color and texture.** Ask yourself if the container will in any way detract from the blooms or arrangement. Heavily patterned and colored vases look lovely with a mass of yellow daffodils or red parrot tulips but will compete with arrangements that have diverse colors, textures, and shapes. Experiment with pretty porcelain cups, etched glass decanters, old or odd-shaped urns, perfume bottles, or metal cans and canisters.

* **Make sure stems have support.** If necessary, your container should have enough space to hold floral tape crisscrossed over the top, floral foam or chicken wire in the bottom, or a metal frog.

above A selection of containers in all shapes and sizes is important for any gardener to have on hand.

Establish and Repeat Tropical Floral Motifs throughout the Room

Gaze heavenward through the glass roof of your garden room and see the tropical sky—it's anywhere you want it to be. The illusion of a tropical night is made more believable by a lush, leafy canopy with trees in tubs and palms in pots all around the room. Paint their containers to look like stalks of bamboo or blooms of ginger tied with string. Situate blooming birds-of-paradise in areas where you want to eliminate dead space or create drama. Soften the angles of the room and windows with round or oval glass-topped tables. Allow ferns and anthuriums to show off beneath. Float giant blooms of hibiscus in clear, glass bowls to reveal the sparkling water as well as the entire flower. Add bamboo and floral motifs (using any of the flowers listed above)—whether carved, molded, painted, or otherwise fashioned—on tables and chairs, lamps, and wall sconces.

Use Art, Color, and Furniture of the 1950s

With colors appropriate for the 1950s, stencil, paint, or decoupage Hawaiian images, including palms, pineapples, fish, vanda orchids, poinciana, Hawaiian maidens, and canoes, onto long, low cabinets that fit beneath windows. Create or purchase flower pots and framed prints featuring island floral art of, for example, sensuous red hibiscus and virginal white or yellow ginger blooms. Choose wall colors in soft yellow-green, beach-sand gold, warm brown, sunset orange, or the crayon pink of that famous grand dame of hotels in the 1950s, the Royal Hawaiian Hotel, also known as Waikiki's Pink Palace. Add furniture made of monkey pod, teak, rattan, or cane.

Track down vintage Hawaiian shirt fabrics and give them new life as pillow coverings or chair throws. Decoupage them onto wooden picture frames. Use them to cover a keepsake memento board. Crisscross the board with grosgrain ribbon and attach picture postcards of the islands.

Buy new fabrics in retro Hawaiian floral motifs to make curtains and chair slipcovers. Trim everything in thick cotton fringe. Find and hang art prints of hula dancers and lei-bedecked ukulele players. Add lamps, ceramic bowls, or trays with images of sugar cane and coconut palm or pictures of Polynesian women going about their daily lives in the *pake muu*, the *holomu*, and the *holoku* (names for various styles of the muu-muu).

Paint shelves in mossy green and stencil or paint images of favorite Hawaiian floral blooms, including *ulu*, the Hawaiian word for breadfruit; *pua melia*, or plumeria, which is frequently strung in flower leis; and *lokelani*, the royal rose. Enhance the feeling of the tropics with natural-fiber floor coverings. Add cotton rugs with flowers and other botanical images that tie into the tropical garden theme. Hang a red cotton or silk quilt that's covered with appliquéd blooms of *kokia keokeo*, or native white hibiscus. The bloom has soft white petals around a stunning red spike.

Use corrugated tin as an angled cornice to resemble a roof over each of your windows and cover the tin in a repeating motif featuring one of the many varieties of heliconias found in the islands. This flower is widely used in island floral arrangements and is unusual in the way that the flower grows out of the plant's main stem and then hangs down. You might also grow ivy vines up and over the little window roofs.

In frames of bamboo, hang tropical landscapes, images of Polynesian fishermen in front of thatched huts or spear fishing from boats, or Hawaiian shirts with coconut buttons. Write Hawaiian words in floral script on metal plant containers, storage drawers, or a garden bench. Add scented candles in coconut shells. Can't you almost hear the trade winds whispering the legends of the *menehune* (island sprites similar to Ireland's leprechauns) over the rhythmic lapping of the surf?

Transform the Ordinary into the Extraordinary with Details

We most often think of garden rooms as ground floor spaces that open out into nature. However, it is possible that you may have a potential garden room on another level. If your home has a screened-in porch, an enclosed balcony or attic, or even a mudroom with lots of windows and plenty of light, it may be possible to convert the space into a dazzling interior garden room with color, garden accents, and lots of flowers.

Determine Function First

How are you going to use the room? Wall color, furnishings, additional lighting, floor materials, window coverings, and accents will be determined by your answer. In some situations, the garden room décor will be dictated by the configuration of the room from which it transitions. If you are unsure about color, try a palette that relies on greens and yellows. Greens, in particular, help the eye transition directly from the garden room straight into nature. Notice in the pictures how these rooms use green and yellow—the most predominate colors in all gardens.

above The gray-green color in this garden tearoom establishes a serene ambience, whereas a judicious use of yellow adds invigorating contrast. Glass in the wall construction and in the French doors provides garden views, rain or shine.

opposite Yellow walls and ceiling work well as a backdrop for green fern fronds and floral motifs throughout this garden room with a view.

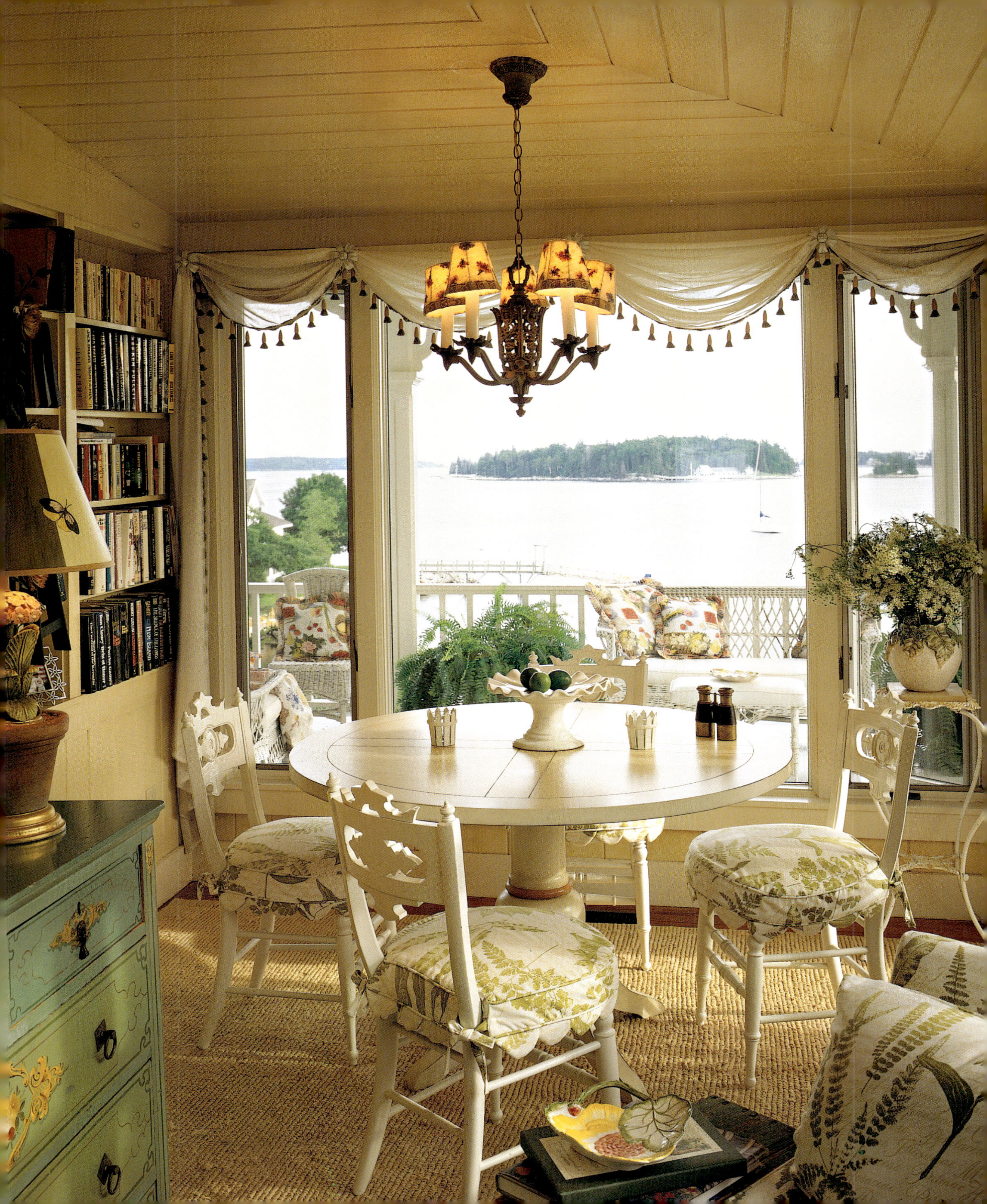

Create a Classical Style

While there are many ways to achieve a classical style, here is a simple technique using two elements—pale, lemon-colored walls and living citrus plants in Italian terra-cotta pots, baskets, or moss-covered stone urns. Put the plants in a formal arrangement (an equal number along each wall, for example). This immediately establishes a classical element. Take the color cues for furnishing the rest of the room from the subdued yellow walls, the quiet green of the leaves and moss, and the ancient earthen colors of the pots or urns. To these two elements, you can then add formal furniture and tailored accents.

Achieve a Casual Look

Create an informal or casual look in four steps. Paint walls with white or pale hues of earth colors. Cover chairs with slipcovers in soft, dreamy pastels in solids or country floral patterns. Add fresh wildflowers, lisianthus, or sweet peas in loose arrangements or put galvanized pots or baskets of lavender and other herbs throughout the room. Toss gardening magazines onto tables and stack herbal and gardening how-to books randomly around the room on plant stands and shelves.

* * * * * * * * * * * * *

right, top *This room has both formal and informal elements. Notice how the pairings—two large mirrors, two tall plant stands holding identical plants, two candles in identical glass holders, two sets of coordinated pillows, two potted ferns, and two glass doors—create a sense of balance and formality while the ruffled table cloth and chairs are more informal.*

right, bottom *The color white seems to disappear, allowing the earth tones of the furniture, the soft, pastel-patterned fabrics, and the many shades of green beyond the French doors to emerge in this enchanting, easy-to-live-in garden room.*

above *Bulbs that have been forced to bloom create seasonal color in late winter or early spring.*

How to Grow Flowers and Plants Indoors

Narcissus, tulips, daffodils, or hyacinth do well in commercial bulb-mix potting soil or in one part sand to three parts compost. Bulbs grown this way need good drainage. When the bulb tops shoot up, camouflage the pot top with gardener's moss.

Winter bulbs, ferns, or other small houseplants can thrive in a terrarium. First, mix together potting soil and compost. After the plants are in, add more soil mixture and then cover with a layer of moss. Keep the plants away from draughts and direct heat.

Topiary can be shaped using any number of plants, including ivy, boxwood, azalea, and juniper. Simple shapes are easiest. Try pyramids, spirals, circles, and cones.

Bulbs can be forced to bloom in vases partially filled with colored glass marbles or pebbles. Simply set the bulb on the stones or marbles and add water until the level reaches the base of the bulb.

Begonia, creeping fig, sweet potato, avocado, geranium, pothos, and African violet all grow well from cuttings in containers of water. Herbs like mint and basil work, too. Once the roots are formed, carefully transplant into soil.

Bonsai plants can be sculpted from miniature or dwarf plants.

Flowers through History

Mechanization and Eclectic Tastes Filled Victorian Homes with Anything Floral

Decoration in the Victorian era was as overstuffed as its furniture. Mass production meant that more people could afford every type of household item—and buy more of them. Every style from the past was fair game in this eclectic mélange of things, and Victorians looked all over the globe for inspiration, drawing ideas from Renaissance revival, Gothic, Japanese, Turkish, and Moorish themes. Sometimes the décor could turn weirdly eclectic, as in the "Aztec Renaissance" concoction dreamed up by one designer and featuring an Aztec floral emblem as its motif.

Flower patterns teemed on fabrics, carpets, and wallpaper. With the three-dimensional effect of embossing, blossoms seemed to pop right off the wall. Censers and fresh flower arrangements helped keep rooms fragrant, but there might be just as many imitation bouquets made of wax or shells for purely decorative effect.

The Victorians draped everything with fabric—all of it decorated. They loved paisley, the stylized teardrop shapes surrounded by small flowers and leaves derived from Kashmir shawls. Jacquard looms later mass-produced the patterns cheaply and profusely. Floral needlework spread over rugs, slipcovers, antimacassars, piano cloths, coverlets, lampshades, lambrequins, wall pockets, and lamp mats. Christopher Dresser, writing about design principles in 1873, stipulated that carpets should be "bloomy," or "have the effect of a garden full of flowers." A fully ornamented summer fireplace might hold several elaborate floral arrangements inside the fender. New synthetic dyes opened up undreamed of color vistas with shades not found in nature—shades some highbrows found appalling. Inexpensive chromolithography provided a cheap way to add color to a room, and many of these prints portrayed idyllic garden scenes.

❀ ❀ ❀ ❀ ❀ ❀ ❀ ❀ ❀ ❀ ❀ ❀ ❀ ❀ ❀ ❀ ❀

opposite *Interior of Linden Hall, formerly the home of F. W. Andreason in Ferndale, California. Victorian decorators divided a wall into three parts, the dado, filling, and frieze, and were not shy about filling every square inch with unmatched, yet related, patterns. Somehow, they made it work.*

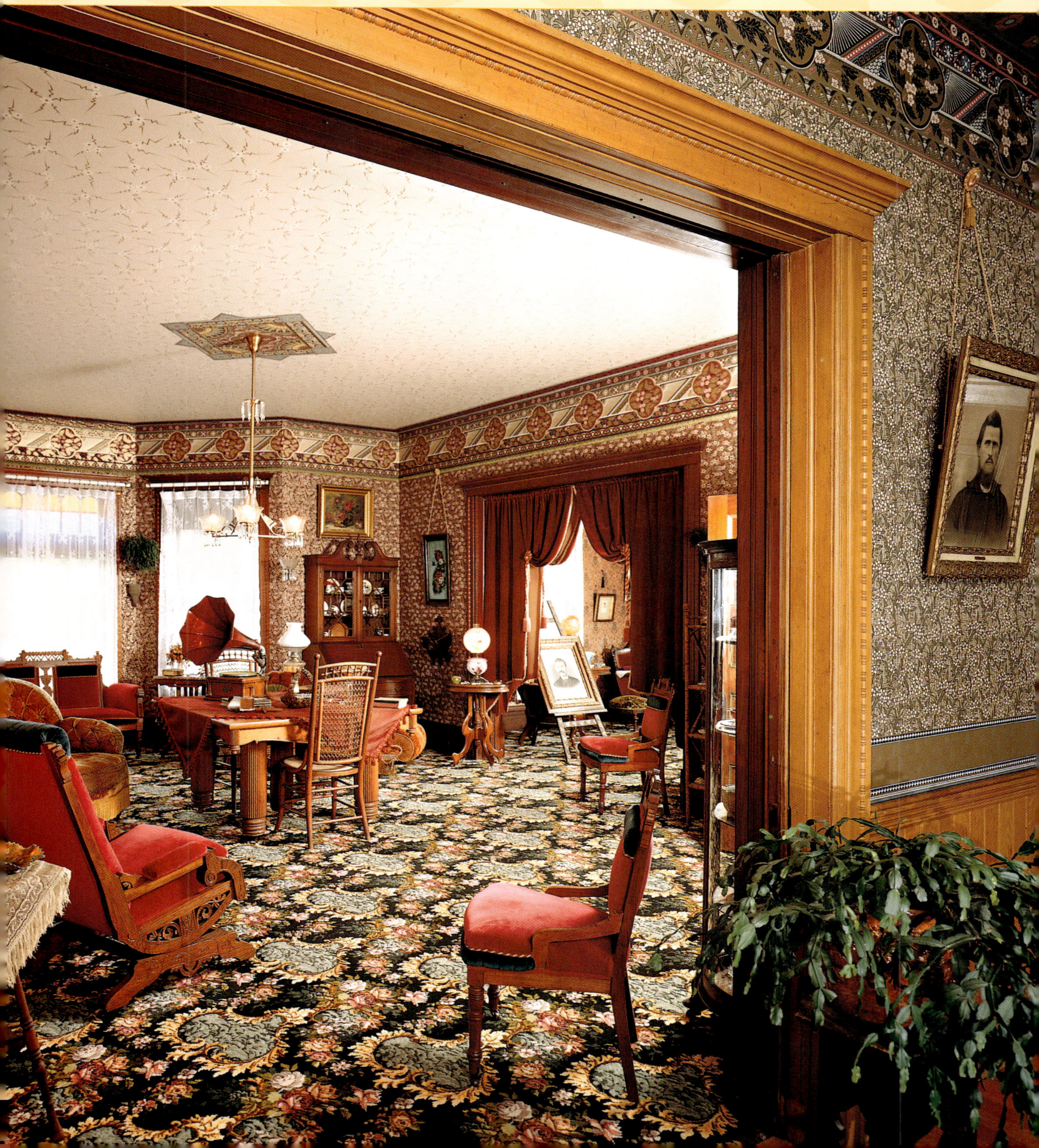

Blooming Accents & Accessories

*There are always flowers for
those who want to see them.*

~ Henri Matisse

It's the Details That Make a Blooming Room Your Own

The hard work is done. The walls are painted, the curtains hung, and the furniture selected. Now the fun begins! Finishing touches like lamps, cushions, rugs, pottery, candlesticks, and art infuse a room with your particular personality and style. When the details are right, you know it instantly. Everyone has a tale of spotting that one perfect item in precisely the right color to complete a room. A great deal of decorating satisfaction derives from just such happy serendipity.

In centuries past, entire rooms—even homes—were done in one style, with furniture, fabrics, and ornamentation matching down to the last detail. Today there's less compulsion for such uniformity. The goal is to create a livable, coherent assemblage, not a severe museum piece or a room that resembles a tag sale's worth of unrelated items. Remember to give a few carefully selected and positioned objects enough elbow room so that the particular qualities of each can be admired. Look for those unexpected juxtapositions—the ornate china and crystal on a rustic table or the antique chair on a modern rug—that inject a note of surprise and humor and make the room truly your own.

opposite Tiles add color to an elegant white fireplace and meld the piece with the rest of the décor. Soft blue paint highlights lines and details on furniture that otherwise might be overlooked.

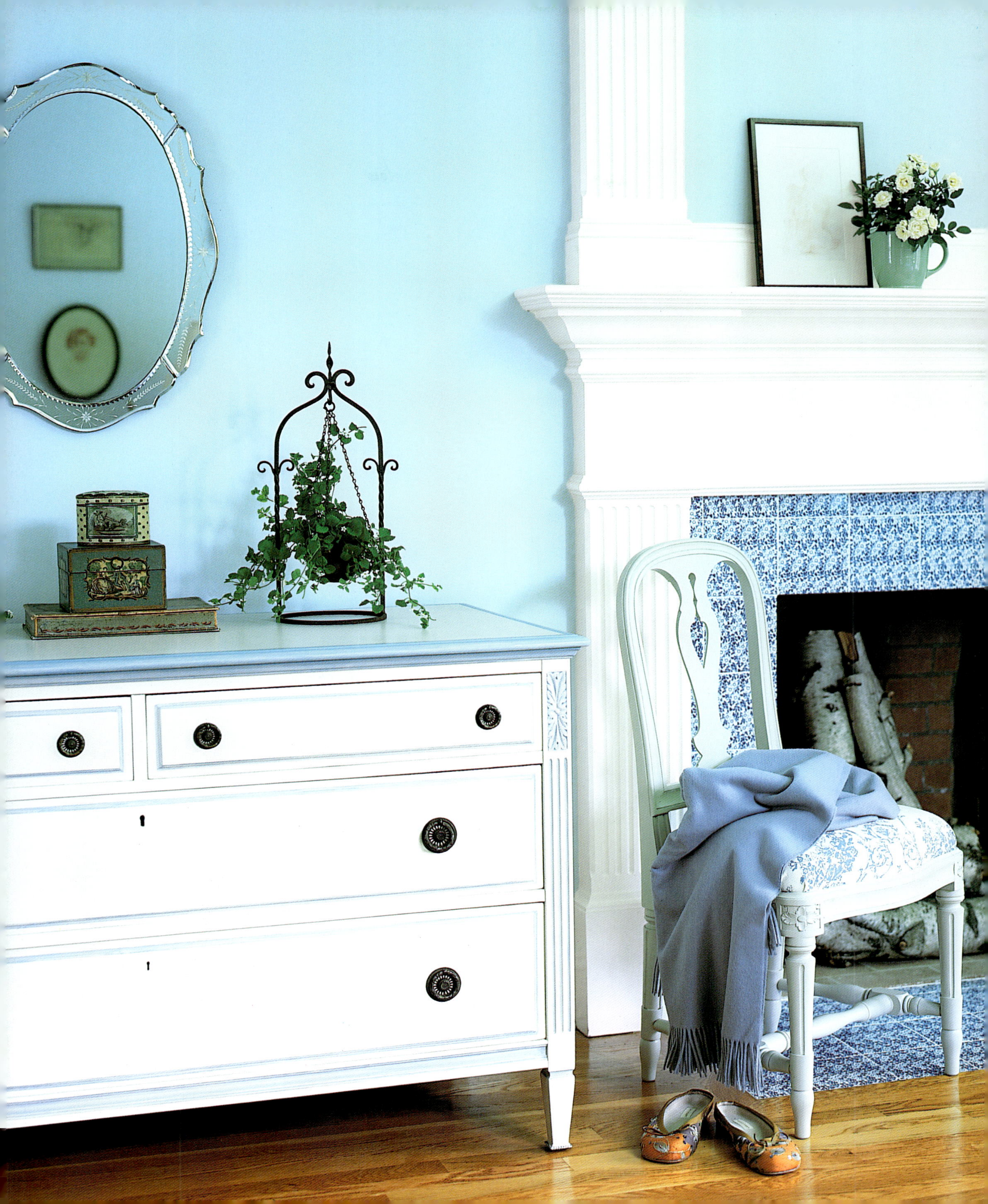

Change the Look of an Item to Get the Effect You Want

There's no rule that says one thing can't look like something else. A little paint and ingenuity can turn walls into gardens, tiles into bouquets, or linoleum into rugs. Is a piece of furniture a little boring? Spruce it up with salvaged trims or carvings, or give it a new face with tile or paint. Scraps and bolts of inexpensive floral fabrics can become slipcovers or new upholstery for furniture, as well as placemats, napkins, curtains, or pillows. Sew pieces of damaged rugs or remnants of vintage floor-cloths in a border around a new, solid-color panel to give old rugs new life. A folding screen can change the look of a room instantly, as well as cover architectural anomalies or disguise a messy desk in the corner.

Change the Function of an Item to Add Character to a Room

Part of the fun of decorating is finding an innovative use for something that might be outside its usual context, an item that someone else no longer wants, or an object that may be missing a part but is still functional. Experiment with garden furniture in the dining room, a chandelier in the kitchen, curtains as tablecloths, a quilt as a sofa slipcover, or a crystal dish to hold soaps in the bathroom. Glue photographs in the centers of orphaned, floral-patterned saucers and arrange them on plate stands on a table. No money for a Monet? Arrange a collection of painted, printed, or embroidered Japanese fans on the wall. Mat and frame floral greeting cards, tiles, or fabric remnants. Assemble a centerpiece of bud vases with mismatched salt and pepper shakers, inkwells, cups, creamers, or eggcups.

right *Painted designs can turn a small cabinet from lovely into spectacular, or a tub into a bower.*

above *Grace a nondescript corner with a charming tromp l'oeil basket for a flower arrangement that can be enjoyed all year long. The delicate fronds visually link the wall pocket, plates, and other decorative details.*

Blooming Accents and Accessories

above *Delicate floral tracery echoes in glassware, tablecloth, and the Victorian birdcage. Such ornate cages are beautiful on their own and can also enclose flower arrangements or candles.*

Find Flowers Everywhere, from Flea Markets to Mega-malls

Once you start looking for flowers, you'll find them everywhere—and they are everywhere. Department stores and linen outlets have done a lot of the work for you by grouping coordinating patterns and colors so you can't go wrong.

Branch out on your own, too. Look through travel magazines and old books for flowers you'll never see blooming in your neighborhood, and let the exotic flora spark your imagination. Architectural salvage lots are rich sources of floral imagery from the past, whether you fancy carved moldings, column capitals, light fixtures, mirror and picture frames, stair railings, or garden gates. Import shops hold a treasure trove of unique flowers from around the world depicted on folk art, embroidered fabrics, saris and shawls, lanterns, furniture, and boxes.

Expect the unexpected. One shop at a California car wash (yes, a car wash!) offers an astounding array of goods, including beaded floral lampshades and padded hangers embellished with silk flowers. You name it, you can find it with a floral theme.

One afternoon of cruising discount stores, department stores, on-line auctions, consignment shops, drug stores, and flea markets yielded the following floral items. And these are just one petal's worth of an entire garden of ideas that you'll find once you start exploring for just the right items for your blooming rooms.

- Spanish amber recycled glass candleholder shaped like a lily
- Cream-colored shadowbox frame tightly packed with red rosebuds beneath glass
- Pewter drawer handles molded into a string of daisies
- Round ceramic knobs painted with yellow and white flowers
- Wine goblets hand-painted with impressionistic flowers
- Roseville pottery lamp with a white primrose design
- Every kind of ceramic floral plate, platter, and bowl imaginable
- Flower-bedecked vases and umbrella stands
- Rose-shaped, cast-iron drawer pulls
- Distressed wooden plant holder with a raised tin flower and leaves

- Peruvian hand-crafted floral mirror frames
- Cast iron doorstop shaped like a basket of flowers
- Tiny topiaries made of dried flowers, baskets, corn grass, and ribbon
- Sachets with flowers tied on top
- Thai wood frames painted with lotus blossoms

right *Someone else's castoff side table can become your charming accent, as well as a plant stand and storage.*

A beautiful, floral porcelain sugar bowl or teapot that has lost its lid becomes a nightlight with the addition of a battery-operated candlestick lamp. Paper parasols decorated with flowers can disguise bare bulbs or unattractive ceiling fixtures. Victorian fluted-glass light shades look like luminous upturned flowers when grouped holding votive candles.

Gorgeous brocade placemats make quick curtains for a small window. Frame several vintage floral handkerchiefs into a wall quilt or stitch a line of them onto cotton backing for a bed skirt. Try an old bedspread refashioned as a shower curtain. Stand a rustic wooden ladder in a corner and hang the rungs with vintage or new floral scarves, shawls, towels, or folded fabric pieces. Sumptuous floral bedding doesn't have to stay in the bedroom. Simple slipcovers for dining room chairs can be fashioned from pillowcases and trim.

Salvaged exterior doors with etched glass or carved swags and rosettes can be refinished and refitted for interior use. Or add a mirror panel and a small shelf to a door to create a unique plant stand. Carved architectural motifs from the capitals of columns, applied decorations, or molded plaster pieces add age and interest to a room when set on shelves or showcased in alcoves. An ornate metal gate gains new status as a headboard or fireplace screen.

above *Intricate mosaics of flowers by artist Teresa Mills add charm and color to a collection of small frames.*

left *Four identically framed prints add a bold graphic element to a dining space where one would seem insufficient. Metal furniture echoes the graceful arch of the Kentia palm, while delicate lines and glass keep the space airy and light.*

opposite *Multiply the patterns, pillows, and accessories to create a room that fairly begs guests to linger over coffee and conversation.*

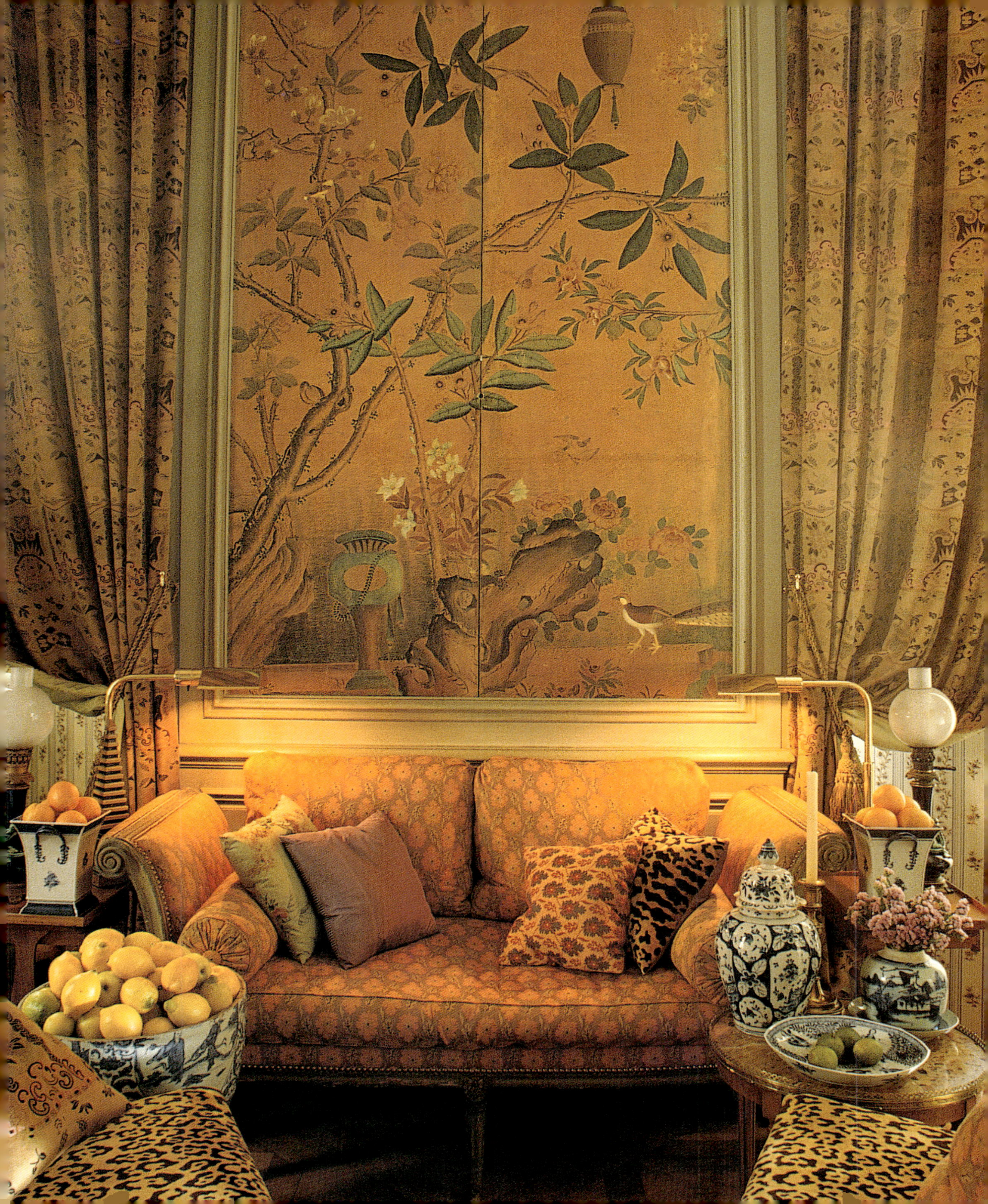

left *Harmonious tones of yellow, blue, and white tie the place settings, trivets, art, and walls together. Color, theme, and artist unify the paintings, while the variously shaped plates and serving platters on the walls share a common pattern.*

bottom left *The furniture doesn't have to be covered in flowers; it can be a flower, like Masanori Umeda's glorious armchair, "Getsuen."*

bottom right *For parties, you can adorn glassware with temporary latex-paint flowers. For permanent embellishment, choose glass already etched or painted with the flower of your choice.*

left When gathered together, paintings, fabrics, and objects with a similar theme, color, or style seem inseparable.

below In centuries past, English nobility could afford solid silver flower arrangements for their winter dinner parties. While much less extravagant, this pot of china orchids looks far more lifelike—and no watering is necessary.

Multiply the Impact with Groups of Objects

One plate looks lonely, but a dozen plates with a similar theme or color, grouped on a wall, make a statement. Similarly, not just one, but mounds of comfy pillows invite repose. You don't need a matched accumulation of expensive pottery to reap the benefits of a collection. Even inexpensive items gather strength in numbers.

Pull together a bouquet of small botanical prints or hanging bud vases on the wall. Array mismatched, colored glass bottles on a table with one bright bloom in each. Assemble vintage silver flatware and serving pieces in floral patterns that you like. Group a few pieces each in several small shadow boxes and hang them as art.

Unify the Whole through Color or Motif

Disparate objects seem to belong together when they're related by a common color scheme, similar pattern, or shared theme. A coordinated palette of one, two, or three colors can hide architectural anomalies, blend old and new elements together, and meld patterns and textures into a unified whole. Whether your taste runs to romantic, contemporary, ethnic, or historic, no one will notice that the furniture comes from different eras when it's garbed in harmonious coats of paint and upholstery.

Choose a flower and look for it everywhere. Fabrics, china, and wall coverings are easy, but don't forget to look at lamp finials, switchplates painted or embossed with borders of roses, metal drawer pulls and cabinet handles molded in flower shapes, ceramic ones painted with blossoms, or even an iron doorstop that resembles a basket of flowers.

Flowers through History

Motifs of the Past Inspired Arts and Crafts Floral Patterns

One reaction to Victorian decorative excess was the Arts and Crafts movement. In the late 19th century, William Morris led a return to quality craftsmanship as he designed and made handcrafted tiles, ceramics, glass, fabrics, tapestries, and wallpapers. Drawing on Celtic, Persian, and Byzantine precursors for the floral motifs in cushion covers, embroidery, tapestries, and carpets, he created designs that remain uniquely his own. Morris also found inspiration from his garden at Red House in Kent, England, where he could study the brier roses, yew, and mallow growing outside his door. His first wallpaper, "Trellis," featuring roses, was followed by patterns of daisies, poppies, marigolds, lilies, sunflowers, tulips, and other flowers in intricate profusion. Around 1881, he began dyeing his own textiles and printing chintz patterns of honeysuckle and peonies, giving his colors whimsical names like "pomegranate flower."

In America, Gustav Stickley's Craftsman style popularized patterns of rhododendrons and poppies in bright colors like green and orange. China-painting clubs offered acceptable social activities for late-19th-century ladies, as they painted floral designs on plain china "blanks."

this page *The wallpaper designs of William Morris are still available. One Morris biographer writing in 1898 called the "Daisy" pattern "a marvel of supreme cleverness; and withal one of which the popularity declines no whit as time goes by." Its continued success 100 years later would probably not come as a surprise.*

opposite *William Morris block-printed his designs, like "Birdland Anemone," using animal and vegetable dyes he made himself. He hated the new aniline dyes, which proved unstable and unpalatable to his sense of color.*

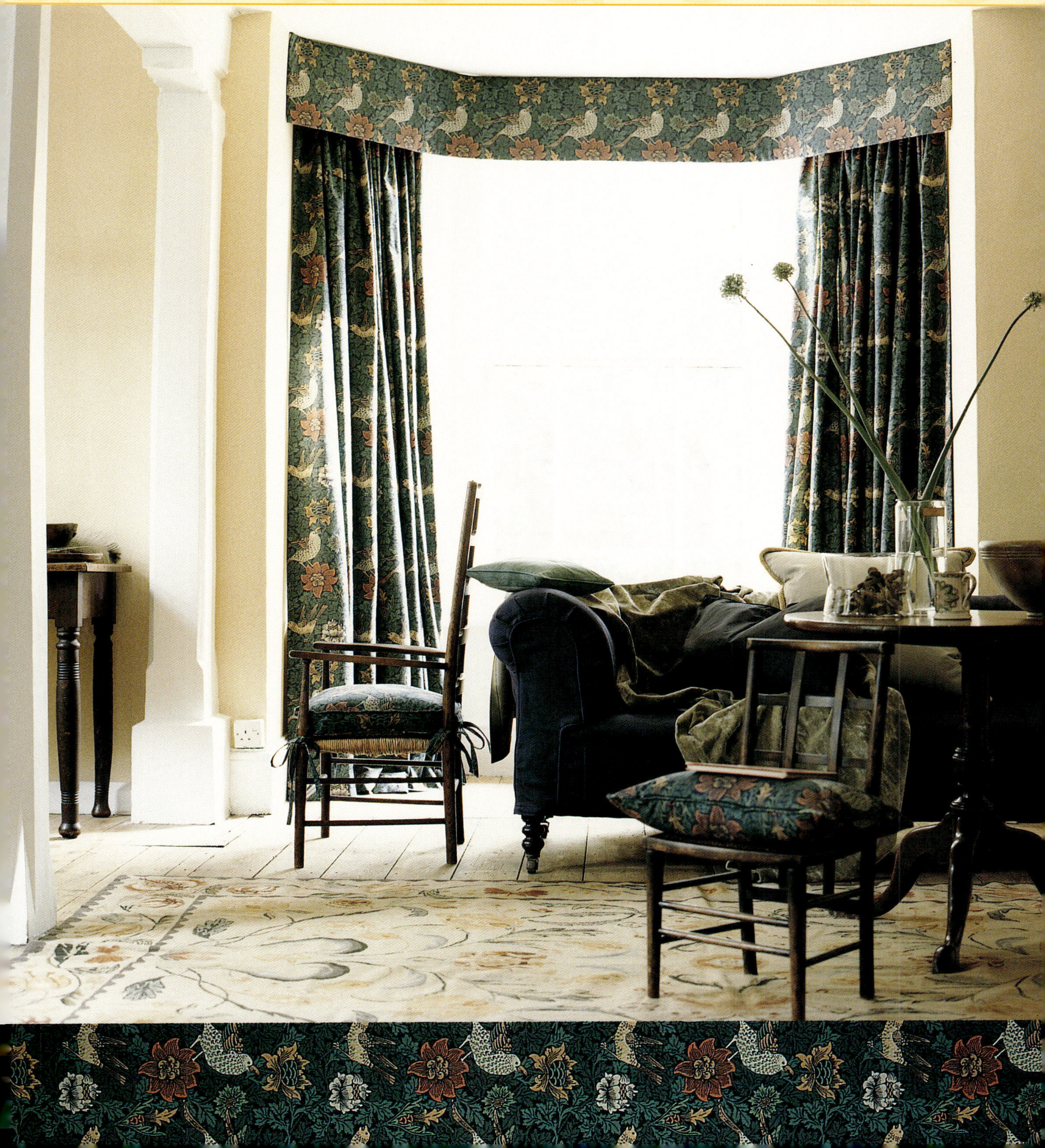

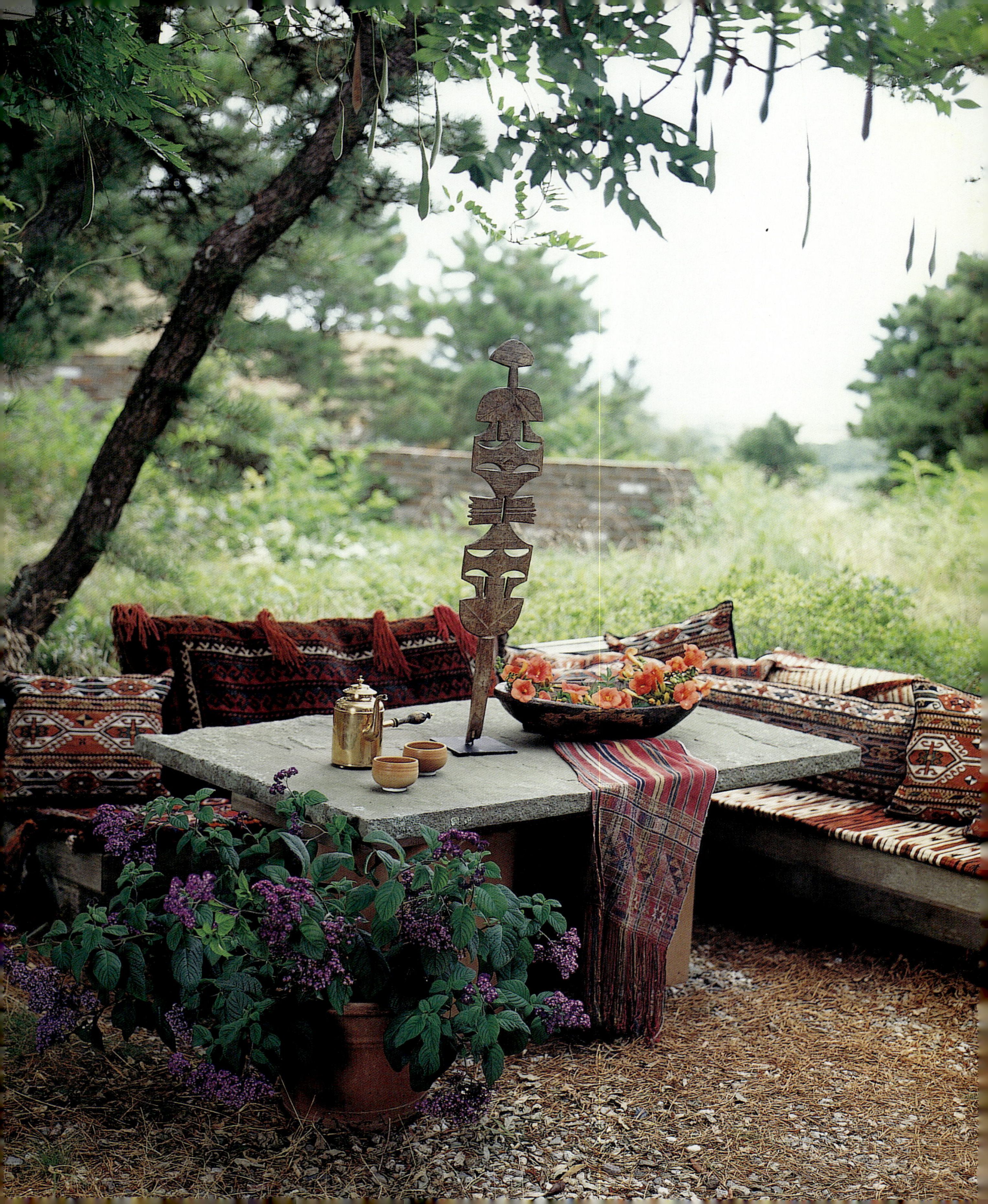

Blooming Outdoor Garden Rooms

*Things flourish,
Then each returns to its root.
Returning to the root is called stillness:
Stillness is called return to Life.*

— Lao-tzu

What could be better than an outdoor room filled with scented blooms, the chatter of birds, and a view of a garden or quiet cove? If the space for a garden room is expansive, it easily accommodates spillover from a large party. If small and intimate, it is the perfect spot for two. Or it can be your own private retreat—a place to laze away the hours watching bees pollinate flowers, squirrels jump from branches, and birds peck at feeders. Here you take tea, ponder ancient questions, and contemplate love and life.

Ideally, an outdoor garden room is a place where harmonious fusion occurs between the natural and human elements. You have to make lots of choices in creating this setting. Begin at the beginning—with the space. Contrary to what you may think, it doesn't have to be much.

❖ ❖ ❖ ❖ ❖ ❖ ❖ ❖ ❖ ❖ ❖ ❖ ❖ ❖

opposite *Here, sheltered by a large jacaranda tree, an outdoor room has been claimed from the wilderness beyond by the addition of a potted plant and vibrantly colored, ethnically patterned textiles along the seating area and over the stone slab table.*

Establish Boundaries, Define the Space

Inevitably, your outdoor garden room will evolve out of your beliefs about the environment, your sense of design, the location and landscape of the space, and its intended use. There are about as many types of spaces that can be turned into outdoor garden rooms as there are plant lovers to create them. Often extending from some type of building, spaces that can be transformed easily into vibrantly colored, heavenly scented retreats from the world include:

- Small terraces, patios, or balconies (where space is quite limited)
- Porches (including verandas and small entry areas)
- Concrete slabs (for suburban houses)
- Walled terraces of stone or wood (for certain types of homes)
- Bare lots (often part of a parcel with a dwelling)
- A flat roof (most often found on city dwellings)

If you want just a small space where you can read and soak up the sun, but all you have is the roof of your apartment building, here's a simple solution. Add two trellises attached to flower boxes. Plant them with blooming vines, and voila! You have walls. Put in three, and you have a room. Want hummingbirds? Plant pots of fuchsia, bee balm, or four-o'clocks. How about butterflies? Plant flowering tobacco, black-eyed Susan, and butterfly bush. Add a beach chair, a bag of books, and buckets of blooms—sun-loving plants with splashy color such as sweet alyssum, French marigold, daylily, coreopsis, daisy, chrysanthemum, petunia, rose mallow, yarrow, zinnia, salvia, verbena, phlox, geranium, and poppy, to name a few—and you have just created a stunning sunning spot.

If your space is a narrow, shady corridor between two buildings, then it is already well defined. But there is still much you can do to enhance the beauty and your enjoyment of that space. Put in shade-loving plants such as impatiens, primrose, violet, lady's mantle, and creeping phlox for spring color; hellebore, astilbe, and foxglove for summer color; foliage plants such as hosta, fern, and ornamental grass; and shrubs like small varieties of rhododendron and camellia. Grow herbs, including mint, oregano, chervil, and parsley (those that flourish in the shade). If you love roses and absolutely must have them, then select shade-tolerant miniatures, a climber like Madame Alfred Carrière (blush-white blooms with a lovely tea-rose fragrance) or a floribunda such as Gruss an Aachen (with blooms that are a delectable apricot pink), all varieties that flower readily in the shade. Put in containers of small trees that you can move around to accommodate their light and water needs. Create a layered look by adding small plants in front of larger ones. Add a fountain and ferns. Hang flat-sided wall pots of blooming lobelia. Put up a trellis. Fasten to it garden art, decorative mirrors, and pretty pots with trailing mint or herbs. Move your bench or chair into position and enjoy.

Make the Most of a View

Does your potential garden room have a great view? Well, as the old adage goes, if you've got it, flaunt it. Select the best vantage point to take in the views and then build your entire room around that spot, even if it is just a balcony. Don't have a spectacular view? Create one. Put in an English cottage garden, an American country garden, or a French potage garden. Make it wild and lushly romantic or manicured and starkly formal, like an English knot garden or one featuring topiaries, parterres, and mazes in shades of green. For a simple approach, plant the flowers you love and add the accents you love to have around, and don't forget to drench the place in scented blooms.

above *Willow and wicker furniture dressed in colorful linen beckon the weary to come sit for a spell amid blooming roses and geraniums in this outdoor room with a view.*

Blooming Outdoor Garden Rooms

above *A painted pergola adorned with lush hanging baskets offers shade, while potted plants on the patio and variegated foliage along the perimeter soften the harsh lines of the redwood fencing.*

Build a Shelter or Plant Some Shade

Trees are ancient providers of shade. Choose a tree and make it the focus. Encircle the trunk with a wraparound seat. Create a stone or concrete floor extending out five or six feet in the shape of a large circle around the tree. Lay a path of stepping-stones (tiled in your favorite floral motifs, of course) from the tree to your house. Line the path with scarlet pelargoniums. Hang a wind chime, put up a floral banner, mount a whirly-gig on a stake, hang tea-light lanterns. With fragrant plants, put in a circular blooming border around the stone floor. Position the shortest plants next to the stones, those of medium height in the middle, and the tallest plants at the back of the bed. For their perfume, choose sweet violet, garden peony, phlox, lavender, red valerian, scented pelargonium, tuberose, and lots of lilies.

No room for a large tree? Plant small patio trees in wine barrels cut in half or large terra-cotta pots. Or put in a painted arbor. Plants still taking up too much space? Construct a large, intricate trellis seat ensconced in a frame with sides, back, and ceiling. Over the top, plant purple wisteria, scarlet clematis, pink jasmine, or fragrant, creamy-colored honeysuckle. If you prefer roses, choose scented, climbing varieties, including Zephirine Drouhin (a fragrant, pink bourbon rose), Lady Banks (covered with buttery yellow, delicately fragrant, tiny roses), or repeat-flowering New Dawn (which produces a multitude of sweetly fragrant, pink blooms). Or put in a pergola. Hang baskets of red begonia, scented white and pink geraniums, or scarlet dianthus and wine-colored fuchsia.

Does your outdoor space enter a desert or an arid field of rocks and wildflowers? Put up a full-size tepee or pitch a Bedouin tent. Fill it with herb-scented pillows. Surround it with containers of plants that thrive in hot, dry climates. Incorporate the stones from the field into this unique space in a way that makes them seem organic to both the landscape and architecture of the outdoor room. Use them to create seating, a fountain, or a permanent planter. Paint flowers on them and use them decoratively.

If you have a simple slab of concrete that is hot as blazes in the summer and you have no space for a full-size tree, plant dwarf or semi-dwarf specimens in half barrels or pots to cool the patio. Install a gazebo or pergola. Or make a canopy out of a gauzy floral fabric that you've hand-blocked, dyed, or tie-dyed yourself. For special occasions, sew a silky floral canopy embellished with your favorite flowers or herbs appliquéd at the center. Tie the canopy to four strong bamboo poles anchored equal distances apart in the ground. This looks heavenly over a stone terrace where the spaces between stones are planted with sedum or moss. Add buckets of fresh flowers. Move a table into position. Set the table with hand-painted, floral dessert plates to hold homemade berry ice cream and krumkake wafers in summer and scones and orange-rosemary jelly in autumn.

A market umbrella anchored to a patio table adds European charm to a courtyard. Be sure to put a vase with a bud on the table every day. Around the courtyard, place tall, metal pots with masses of blooms. Paint the words for garden from your favorite foreign language on the sides of the containers.

For long narrow porches, consider a colorful awning with a scalloped, fringed, or straight edge to add a finished look. Hang tin pocket containers on walls and fill them with luxurious, brilliantly colored blooms. Paint or write the names of different flowers on each.

Want shelter or shade that's a little more elaborate? Add a small garden shed. Today's manufacturers offer everything from a standard little building to a stunning English cottage or American Colonial retreat—complete with cupola. Paint it green, periwinkle blue, or gray (if you want the flower and foliage colors around it to take center stage). Plant lemon-scented roses alongside. Write garden poetry across the outside surfaces. Illustrate with a plethora of pastel petunias, pansies, poppies, and sweet peas. Create a memory on its walls. Write in gold or silver ink the name of a beloved. Paint and press your child's hand on an exterior wall. Allow him or her to write the family name. String up a hammock. Pull over an Adirondack chair or rocking chair. Plant an herbaceous border or a scented garden nearby. Add a chorus of color in pots near the shed door. Paint an old farm chair and put a pot of blooming geraniums on the seat.

Make It Special with Accents, Details, and Lighting

Wrap wire around the necks of old canning jars. Cover the wire with a short skirt of calico or heavy cotton lace. Tie with ribbon or twine. Fasten the extending pieces of wire to screws in garden shed walls. Add water and bouquets.

Hang a trellis on a wall and display old sunbonnets and straw gardening hats. Sow geraniums in an old wheelbarrow. Make display shelves from two weather-beaten, hinged ladders by placing boards across the steps. Display garden artifacts such as an antique twine dispenser and an old washbasin and pitcher. In a wire basket, put bars or petal leaves of homemade soap (lavender, lemon, aloe, rose) in see-through sachet bags tied with ribbon. On a gardener's workbench, place a crate to display containers of seed and scented gardener's salve over a bed of dried stems (lemon grass or lavender). Set out old canning jars, pickle crocks, and sap buckets. Fill them with fresh blooms.

For outdoor parties, decoupage pictures from seed catalogs onto flowerpots of citronella candles to add light and keep away mosquitoes. Arrange tiki lamps or hang Asian or ornamental garden lamps on shepherd's hooks. Dress garden tables with old linens, repaired and washed white. Or tile a garden table and serve a summer bounty on flower-embellished china adorned with edible blooms.

top *Neutral white serves as the perfect foil for the bold splashes of color in the floral-patterned pillows and hanging baskets.*

bottom *A table with green tiles makes a lovely surface on which to serve salad adorned with freshly picked, edible nasturtiums.*

How to Dry and Press Flowers, Drawing Inspiration from the Seasons for Blooms All Year Long

Dry your flowers after picking them at their peak. Strip the leaves. Tie them to a hanger, hook, or line singly or in small bunches and hang them upside-down in a dark place until dry. Recondition through the night by placing a drying agent such as sand, silica gel, or borax in a 1" (2.5 cm) layer in an airtight plastic container. Place flower heads on the agent, being careful not to let the flower heads touch each other. Sift the silica gel over the flowers until they are lightly covered. Cover and seal the box lid with tape. Check the flowers after 24 hours. Usually they are ready within two days.

Press flowers using a commercially available flower press, or make one from a board, paper (newsprint or thin, utilitarian art paper), silica gel, paper towels, and a weight (books, heavy pan, bricks). Place the paper on the board. Sprinkle with a layer of silica gel. Cover the gel with a paper towel. Position flowers and foliage on the towel. Then simply reverse the steps. Slip the stack into resealable plastic bag. Squeeze out the air. Cover with a heavy weight. Wait seven to ten days before removing and using your pressed flowers.

Preserve herbs such as lavender and rosemary by air-drying and then use them in wreaths, potpourri, and sachet bags. Hydrangea flower heads from summer can be air-dried for enjoyment in arrangements during late fall and winter.

Dry soft-petal blossoms such as pansies, sweet peas, and freesias in the spring and marigolds, zinnias, poppies, cosmos, gaillardia, nasturtiums, pelargoniums, and dahlias in the summer at the peak of their bloom to brighten a kitchen or other areas of the home when the snow is falling.

Air-dry tiny rosebuds and tie them into a garland or in bunches with colorful ribbon. Create rosebud and shadow-box pictures, or place the buds in small vases or a candy dish at your bedside to enjoy when December winds are howling.

Snip branches of plum, apricot, and willow along with wisteria or grape vines during pruning season. Fashion wreaths and garlands upon which to glue dried flowers and foliage, herbs, nuts, and seedpods for enjoyment in other seasons.

Use soft, colorful petals in homemade paper cards for friends throughout the year.

Flowers through History

Art Nouveau Embraced Fantastical Flower and Tendril Motifs

At the turn of the 20th century, the sinuous curves of Art Nouveau captured the sensuality of nature in all its floral and flowing forms. Designers mimicked and "improved" nature in every medium available. Tracing its roots back to Celtic, Gothic, Rococo, and Japanese decorative arts, the style was a curvilinear, organic response to the straight, clean lines of the Arts and Crafts and Mission styles.

Art Nouveau can justly be called a movement obsessed with flowers, and its purveyors had no problem gilding the lily. Gold floral patterns shimmered on moiré wall fabric, blue irises curved up pink glass, chandeliers blossomed with petals, water lilies gleamed on pewter plaques, and richly colored roses snaked around table linens. Flowing-haired women emerged bare-breasted from foliage-covered clocks and lamps garlanded with irises and poppies. Flowers of brass, copper, and mother-of-pearl surrounded picture frames. Wrought iron gates sprouted rhythmic tendrils. Flower forms proliferated across carpets, upholstery, pottery, furniture, and fire screens as wood and glass seemed to grow with convolvulus, thistledown, and fragile purple honesty. Even such mundane items as drawer pulls couldn't escape cascades of floral embellishment.

Simple Folk Motifs Continued the Floral Tradition

Scandinavian and Eastern European immigrants brought to America their traditions of beautifully woven textiles, including chair cushions embroidered with delicate sprigs, coverlets woven with stylized rosettes, and fabrics dotted with fuchsia, tulips, or vases of blossoms. Flowers remained a staple of folk art and homespun crafts, with simple shapes that were easy to execute, yet always beautiful.

Contemporary Florals Look to the Past—and the Future

In the 1930s, machine-age motifs predominated, but modern, stylized flower shapes melded with the streamlined Art Deco style. A proliferation of new fabrics and plastics meant that just about anything could be molded into, or printed with, flower shapes.

Young people in the 1960s weren't called the Flower Generation for nothing. Along with peace, love, and music, the decade was abloom with psychedelic flower designs in neon colors, as well as a resurgence of Asian and Indian motifs, including paisley. Anything that was as different as possible from convention (that is, what your parents had) was groovy. Who can forget those giant Pop Art daisies—especially since they've recently made a comeback?

The 1970s saw a resurgence of Victorian floral patterns in Laura Ashley's fabrics. Today, flowered wallpaper patterns dating back centuries are being revived, and tried-and-true paisley is all the rage once more.

right *Walter Crane used two of the most popular Art Nouveau motifs in his "Flower Fairy" tiles—flowers and the female form, circa 1900.*

opposite, top *This quilt, made in Indiana, features the "Tulips in a Vase" pattern.*

opposite, bottom *The Art Nouveau style is epitomized in this salon table crafted in the form of a water lily, circa 1900.*

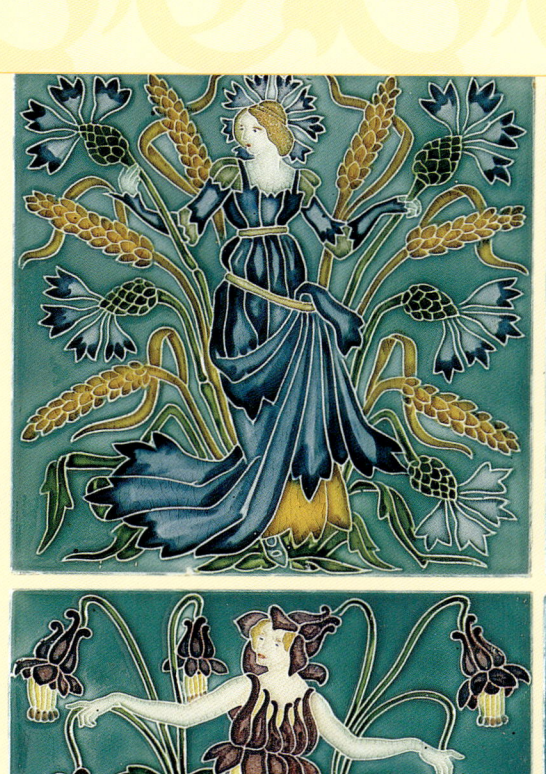

Gardens of Inspiration
A FEW FAMOUS GARDENS FROM AROUND THE WORLD

BELIZE

Belize Botanic Gardens
P.O. Box 180
San Ignacio, Cayo
Belize, Central America
501-824-3101
www.belizebotanic.org

The gardens feature a collection of orchids native to Belize, which has over 300 indigenous species. That number represents one percent of the world's 30,000 species.

CANADA

Royal Botanic Gardens
680 Plains Road West
Burlington, Ontario, L7T 4H4
905-527-1158
www.rbg.ca

Canada's largest botanical garden has five display gardens and four nature sanctuaries on 1,100 hectares.

ENGLAND

Royal Botanic Gardens, Kew
Richmond, Surrey
0-208-332-5000
www.rbgkew.org.uk

The grounds feature the Temperate House and the Kew Palm House, along with a world-famous collection of palm trees.

FRANCE

Chateau de Versailles Orange
78000 Versailles
01-30-84-74-00
www.chateauversailles.fr

This garden at the Royal Palace of Versailles near Paris houses more than a thousand plants, and its orangery dates to Louis XIV.

INDIA

Kolkata Botanical Gardens
Near Howrah Bridge along the west bank of the
Hoogly River
Calcutta, Bengal
866-652-4422
www.allindiatourtravel.com/hot_spots/kolkata/
    botanical_gardens/#1

The gardens, founded in 1786, house over 12,000 plants and many types of exotic botanical specimens including an old banyan tree with the second largest canopy in the world, Cuban palms, multicolored bamboo trees, a double coconut tree from Sicily, and medicinal plants. There are also a botanical library and an orchid house.

JAPAN

Shinjuku Gyoen (National Gardens)
11 Naito-cho
Shinjuku-ku, Tokyo 160-0014
03-3350-0151
www.shinjukugyoen.go.jp/English/English-index.html

The gardens blend three styles: French formal, English landscape, and Japanese traditional. The site stocks more than 2,400 tropical and subtropical species and has more than 2,000 trees.

REPUBLIC OF IRELAND

National Botanic Gardens, Glasnevin
Finglas Road
Glasnevin, Dublin 7
353-1-837-7596
www.mixedpk.com/ireland2002

A Victorian park with an excellent conservatory, the garden features greenhouses from the 19th century, an exceptional orchid collection, tropical trees, cycads, and the Great Palm House.

SINGAPORE

Sentosa Orchid Gardens
33 Allanbrooke Road
Sentosa Island
65-6275-0388
www.sentosa.com/sg/a-orchid.htm

One of many gardens, this island garden features a dazzling collection of tropical orchid varieties, a koi pond, fountains, and a food court.

UNITED STATES OF AMERICA

Golden Gate Park
John F. Kennedy Drive
San Francisco, CA 94117
415-666-7017
www.conservatoryofflowers.org

Newly restored, the Conservatory of Flowers, the oldest wooden glasshouse in the United States, has five display galleries with stunning exhibits ranging from potted plants you'd see in 1880s Victorian England to a Polynesian biology exhibit. It offers ongoing educational exhibits and flower shows.

The New York Botanical Garden
200th Street and Kazimiroff Boulevard
Bronx, New York 10458-5126
718-817-8616
www.nybg.org

The garden has one of the largest Victorian glasshouses in the nation.

The U.S. Botanic Garden
245 First Street SW
Washington, DC 20024
202-225-8333
www.aoc.gov

A house of rare and endangered species and a palm house are maintained here.

WALES

National Botanic Gardens of Wales
Middleton Hall
Llanarthne, Carmarthenshire
01558-668-768
www.gardenofwales.org

This, the first national botanical garden created in the U.K., and the only one for over 200 years, is built on the former 18th-century regency park of Middleton Hall in Carmarthenshire. The Great Glasshouse opened in 2000.

Bibliography

Allen, Oliver E. *Decorating with Plants.* Alexandria: Time-Life Books, Inc., 1978.

Atha, Antony. *Container Gardening: Using Containers to Enhance Your Garden.* Bath: Parragon, 2002.

Ashley, Laura. *Laura Ashley Decorating with Patterns and Textures: Using Color, Pattern, and Texture in the Home.* New York: Crown Publishers, Inc., 1996.

Barnes, Christine, and the editors of Sunset Books. *Colors for Your Home.* Menlo Park: Sunset Publishing Corporation, 1999.

Baster, Fred E., and Charles Phoenix. *Leis, Luaus and Alohas: The Lure of Hawaii in the Fifties.* Waipahu: Island Heritage Publishing, 1999.

Bonar, Ann. *The Complete Guide to Conservatory Plants.* London: Collins & Brown Limited, 1992.

Browning, Marie. *Natural Soapmaking.* New York: Sterling Publishing Co., Inc., 1999.

Brown, Simon. *Practical Feng Shui: Arrange, Decorate, and Accessorize Your Home to Promote Health, Wealth, and Happiness.* London: Cassell Illustrated, 1997.

Burrell, Paul. *In the Royal Manner: Expert Advice on Etiquette and Entertaining from the Former Butler to Diana, Princess of Wales.* New York: Warner Books, 1999.

Chuen, Master Lam Kam. *Feng Shui Handbook: How to Create a Healthier Living and Working Environment.* New York: Henry Holt and Company, 1996.

Clifton-Mogg, Caroline. *Textile Style: The Art of Using Antique and Exotic Fabrics to Decorate Your Home.* Boston, New York, London: Little, Brown and Company, Inc., Aurum Press Ltd., 2001.

Cohen, Sacha. *The Painted Wall: Transforming Your Walls with Stunningly Simple Paint Effects.* Minnetonka: Creative Publishing International, 2001.

De Vleeschouwer, Olivier. *Greenhouses and Conservatories.* Paris: Flammarion, 2000.

Gibb, Helen R. *The Secrets of Fashioning Ribbon Flowers.* Iola: Krause Publications, 1998.

Gilliatt, Mary. *Mary Gilliatt's Interior Design Course.* New York: Watson-Guptill Publications, 2001.

Glovier, Doris. *The Stamped and Stenciled Home: Easy, Beautiful Designs for Walls, Floors, and Home Accessories.* Gloucester: Rockport Publishers, Inc., 2002.

Jones, Owen. *The Grammar of Ornament.* New York: DK Publishing, Inc., 2001.

Jones, Chester. *Colefax and Fowler: The Best in English Interior Decoration.* Boston, New York, Toronto, London: Little Brown and Company Inc., Bulfinch Press, 1989.

Martson, Peter. *Garden Room Style.* New York: Rizzoli International Publications, Inc., 1998.

Martin, Laura C. *Handmade Gifts from a Country Garden.* New York: Abbeville Press, 1994.

Ohrbach, Barbara Milo. *The Scented Room: Cherchez's Book of Dried Flowers, Fragrance and Potpourri.* New York: Clarkson N. Potter, Inc., 1986.

Peebles, Douglas. *A Pocket Guide to Hawaii's Flowers.* Honolulu: Mutual Publishing, 1997.

Pickles, Sheila, ed. *The Fragrant Garden.* New York: Harmony Books, 1992.

Poakalani, and John Serrao. *Poakalani. Hawaiian Quilt Cushion Patterns and Designs, Vol. 3.* Honolulu: Mutual Publishing, 2001.

Roth, Susan A. *Flower Gardening.* Des Moines: Meredith Corporation, Better Homes and Gardens Books, 1995.

Salamony, Sandra, and Maryellen Driscoll. *A Gardener's Craft Companion: Simple Modern Projects to Make with Garden Treasures.* Gloucester: Rockport Publishers, Inc., 2002.

Spours, Judy. *The Ultimate Decorating Book.* London: Collins and Brown, Limited, 1998.

Stabile, Enrica. *Open Air Living, Creative Ideas for Stylish Outdoor Living* New York: Ryland Peters & Small, Inc., 2001.

Straeten, Judith, archivist at Brunschwig & Fils. *Toiles de Jouy.* Salt Lake City: Gibbs Smith, 2002.

Martha Stewart Living Omnimedia LLC. *Arranging Flowers: How to Create Beautiful Bouquets in Every Season.* New York: Crown Publishing Group, Clarkson Potter/Publishers, 1999.

Strong, Roy. *Creating Small Gardens.* New York: Villard Books, 1987.

Wagstaff, Liz. *Paint Recipes: A Step-by-Step Guide to Colors and Finishes for the Home.* San Francisco: Chronicle Books, 1996.

Whitfield, Josephine. *Decoupage, Using Paper to Decorate Your Home.* London: Anness Publishing Limited, Southwater, 2001.

Wilson, Erica. *Crewel Embroidery.* New York: Charles Scribner's Sons, 1962.

Wood, Christopher. *Victorian Painting.* Boston, New York, London: Little, Brown and Company, Bulfinch Press, 1999.

Resources

AMANDA ROSS
Studio 54
Clink Street Studios
1 Clink Street
London SE1 9DG UK
Clink.54@virgin.net
207-234-0832
Handprinted interior textiles, including botanical themes.

ANNA FRENCH LTD.
343 Kings Road
London SW3 5ES UK
171-351-1126

BALDWIN'S BOOK BARN
865 Lenape Road
West Chester, PA 19382 US
www.bookbarn.com
Digital botanical prints on archival paper of every flower imaginable.

COUNTRY CURTAINS
At The Red Lion Inn
P.O. Box 955
Stockbridge, MA 01262 US
800-456-0321
www.countrycurtains.com
Wide variety of curtain styles from period-type curtains to modern country in fabrics ranging from cotton to Battenburg lace, toile, gingham, and silk dupioni, to name a few.

CRISTINA ACOSTA
Cristina Acosta Art Gallery
Old Mill Marketplace
550 Industrial Way #28A
Bend, OR 97702 US
541-388-5157
www.CristinaAcosta.com
Cristina@CristinaAcosta.com
Hand-painted tiles, furniture, and more.

DOMINIC CRINSON/DIGITILE
15 Redchurch Street
London E2 7DJ UK
207-613-2783
www.crinson.com
Digital designs for tile, Formica, vinyl, wall covering, and flooring.

DORIS LESLIE BLAU
724 Fifth Avenue, Sixth Floor
New York, New York 10019 US
212-586-5511
www.dorislieblau.com
Antique carpets and rugs, including Persian, Aubusson, Turkish, and Bessarabian.

FESTIVE FIBERS
P.O. Box 626
Alstead, NH 03602 US
603-825-2247
www.festivefibers.com
One-of-a-kind furniture pieces created with handmade, felt fabric upholstery in beautiful floral designs.

J.P. WEAVER
941 Air Way
Glendale, CA 91201 US
818-500-1740

LAURA ASHLEY LTD.
Freepost
P.O. Box 5
Newtown
POWY5 5Y16 ILK UK
871-230-2301

LIORA LIGHTS
160 Johnson Avenue
Hackensack, NJ 07601 US
201-487-7600
www.lioralights.com
Distributor of wax candle bowls by The Inwater Group, as well as a wide variety of lights and candles, such as wax candles with embedded flower petals and oil- and flower-filled liquid lights.

MARIPOSA
www.mariposa-gift.com
An extensive range of high-end table and giftware ranging from casual to formal.
To the trade only
Dealer locator: 800-788-1304

MOTAWI TILEWORKS
170 Enterprise Drive
Ann Arbor, MI 48103 US
734-213-0017
www.motawi.com
Ceramic art tiles, specializing in Arts and Crafts styles.

PLOW & HEARTH COUNTRY HOME
P.O. Box 619
Madison, VA 22727-0619
800-627-1712
www.plowandhearth.com
Country furnishings, dinnerware, rugs, bedding, curtains, and accessories.

POTTERY BARN
P.O. Box 7044
San Francisco, CA 94120-7044
800-922-5507
www.potterybarn.com
Contemporary furnishings for the home.

RETROUVIUS
2A Ravensworth Road
London NW10 5NR UK
www.retrouvius.com
Solid "wallpaper" from reclaimed marble, travertine, and granite, as well as other products from salvaged materials.

SMITH & HAWKEN
P.O. Box 8690
Pueblo, CO 81008-9998 US
800-776-3336
www.SmithandHawken.com
Everything garden lovers need to fill their homes with blooms, including plants, pots, Victorian hothouses, birdbaths, vases, and garden furniture and art.

STURBRIDGE YANKEE WORKSHOP
Portland, ME 04102 US
800-343-1144
www.sturbridgeyankee.com
Large selection of Shaker and country-style furnishings, curtains, accents, and art.

TERESA MILLS
The Mosaic Place
Brazilian Cottage
86 North Town Road
Maidenhead, Berkshire
SL6 7JH UK
info@themosaicplace.co.uk
Art and frames crafted from hand-painted and hand-cut tile fragments.

TILE SOURCE, INC.
Roswell, GA 30076 US
770-993-6602
www.tile-source.com
Specialists in the supply of ceramic and other materials for restoration.

WAYSIDE GARDENS
1 Garden Lane
Hodges, SC 29695-0001 US
800-845-1124
www.waysidegardens.com
Enormous selection of roses and other plants for the garden.

❀ Online Resources

WWW.ACCENTS-OF-FRANCE.COM
Decorative trellises and accessories for home and garden, including pilasters, planters, obelisks, panels, and more.

WWW.ANNSACKS.COM
Ann Sacks Tile and Stone Co. carries art tiles and metal knobs and pulls with flower motifs, and more.

WWW.ANTIQUE-LINENS.COM
Selection of vintage and antique linens.

WWW.BOMBAYCOMPANY.COM
Home accessories, furniture, and art.

WWW.CALICOCORNERS.COM
Home decorator fabrics.

WWW.CEDARVALE.NET
Essential oils, soapmaking supplies, and herbs, as well as orris root powder, gum tragacanth, and other supplies for making potpourri and scented pastilles.

WWW.CES.NCSU.EDU/HIL/HIL-8513.HTML
Lists edible flowers and descriptions of how they taste.

WWW.CHRISBARRETTDESIGN.COM
Chris Barrett, interior design

WWW.CLASSICREVIVALS.COM
Wallpapers based on 18th- to 19th-century European patterns, silk, cotton, and linen fabrics, as well as handcrafted, embossed leather panels and borders for walls.

Resources

WWW.DRESSLERSTENCIL.COM
Over 600 different stencil designs, as well as paints, brushes, and how-to videos.

WWW.EMENEE.COM
Every sort of flower-shaped handle, drawer pull, and knob you could possibly want.

WWW.FLORALCONCEPTSINTL.COM
All types of dried flowers, including hydrangeas, roses, mosses, lavender, and more.

WWW.GLIDDEN.COM
Inspiration as well as information about interior styles, paint colors, room types, and Glidden brands.

WWW.HANNAHSTREASURES.COM
WWW.SECONDHANDROSE.COM
Both companies stock vintage wallpapers in many floral patterns.

WWW.IKEA.COM, WWW.IKEA-USA.COM, WWW.IKEA-GLOBAL.COM
IKEA offers Scandinavian modern style furniture and accessories for the home. The company operates stores in 34 countries. In the United States, IKEA's stores are located in California, Maryland, Virginia, Texas, New Jersey, New York, Pennsylvania, Washington, and Illinois.

WWW.KOHLER.COM
Ceramic sinks, fixtures, and other accessories, many with floral themes.

WWW.LAURAASHLEY.COM
Textile patterns, wallpapers, furniture, and window coverings for every room in your home.

WWW.LONDONLACE.COM
Furniture, lighting, and linens in classic and contemporary styles.

WWW.MOSAICELEMENTS.COM
Hand-cut ceramic flowers and other objects to add textural and floral elements to lamps, table tops, columnar bases, flower pots, and other pique assiette mosaic works of art for the home.

WWW.PRINTSPAST.COM
On-line gallery and shop of antique botanical and nature prints.

WWW.RENAISSANCE-ONLINE.COM
Conservatories for American homes.

INFO@SANDERSON-US.COM
Sanderson offers classic English floral textiles, including curtains and upholstery as well as accessories for home decorating.

WWW.SHABBYCHIC.COM
This company's flagship store featuring comfortable furnishings and fabrics opened in 1989 in Santa Monica, California. Based on the designs and popular book by Rachel Ashwell, the company now has stores in various California locations, including Santa Monica, San Francisco, Malibu, and Newport Beach as well as in New York and Chicago.

WWW.SPIEGEL.COM
Spiegel is well known for its catalog featuring distinctive home furnishings and accessories.

WWW.THECOUNTRYHOUSE.COM
Antique reproduction furniture, linens, shelving, cabinets, potpourri, tinware, candles, and more.

WWW.VINTAGECLIPART.COM
Authentic Victorian and vintage graphics.

WWW.WICKERHOUSE.COM
Indoor and outdoor wicker furniture, as well as teak, wrought iron, and aluminum, plus many items for bed, bath, and children's rooms.

WWW.ZR-GROUP.COM
Zimmer & Rohde, a German company that features textiles for interiors.

Photography Credits

Sandy Agrafiotis, 40
Courtesy of Amdega/www.amdega.co.uk, 94; 96; 106; 108 (bottom)
Courtesy of Laura Ashley Limited/www.laurashley.com, 9; 15; 74 (top); 120 (bottom right); 139; 141
Chris Barrett Design/www.chrisbarrettdesign.com, 89
Courtesy of Doris Leslie Blau, Inc., 68 (bottom); 79
The Bridgeman Art Library/Grammar of Ornament, Owen Jones, Artist (1809-1874), 64
The Bridgeman Art Library/Palampore coverlet, Indian School, 18th century, 54 (top)
Courtesy of Brunschwig & Fils, 44
Björg, 50
Bobbie Bush Photography/www.bobbiebush.com/Doris Glovier, Artist, 53
Bobbie Bush Photography/www.bobbiebush.com/Sandra Salamony, Artist, 60
Bobbie Bush Photography/www.bobbiebush.com/Sandra Salamony & Maryellen Driscoll, Artists, 131
Courtesy of Dominic Crinson/www.crinson.com, 29 (top)
Guillaume DeLaubier, 29 (right); 57; 69; 72; 100; 103; 109; 116; 119; 120 (top)

Courtesy of Glidden, an ICI Paint company/www.glidden.com, 14; 87; 113
Steve Gross & Susan Daley, 39 (bottom); 43; 70; 86
Reto Guntli, 85
Mick Hales, 24, 61; 81; 91; 115; 130 (bottom)
Mick Hales/Bobby McAlpine, Design, 66
Brian Harrison/Red Cover, 28; 32
Courtesy of IKEA/www.ikea.com, 83 (top)
Al Karevy/Festive Fibers, 48
Douglas Keister, 111
Courtesy of The Kohler Company/www.kohler.com, 60 (bottom)
Erich Lessing/Art Resource, NY, Archaeological Museum, Heraklion, Crete, Greece, 21
Louvre, Paris, France/Réunion des Musées Nationaux, Art Resource, NY, 93
Courtesy of Mariposa/www.mariposa-gift.com, 58 (bottom, left & right); 68 (top); 104; 121 (middle right)
Masanori Umeda Armchair, Getsuen, Produced by Edra S.p.A. (Pisa, Italy), Liliane & David M. Stewart Collection, gift of Maurice Forget/Musée Des Beaux-Arts De Montreal/Giles Rivest, 120 (bottom left)
Gilles Mermet/Art Resource, NY, National Museum of Carthage, Tunisia, 33
Shelley Metcalf, 41; 128
Courtesy of Mosaic Place/www.themosaicplace.co.uk, 118 (right)
Courtesy of Motawi Tileworks/www.motawi.com, 62 (bottom)
Musée des Arts Decoratifs, Paris, France/Giraudon/Art Resource, NY, 132 (bottom left)
Musée du Moyen Age (Cluny), Paris, France/Réunion des Musées Nationaux, Art Resource, NY, 65
The Newark Art Museum, Newark, NJ/Art Resource, NY, 55

The Newark Museum, Newark, NJ/Gift of Mrs. Pearl Grace Loehr Wagner/Art Resource, NY, 132 (top right)
Rob Proctor, illustrator, 90; 97; 98; 99
Courtesy of Retrouvius/www.retrouvius.com, 26 (right, top & bottom)
Courtesy of Amanda Ross, 74 (bottom)
Eric Roth, 31; 36; 38 (top); 49; 76; 124; 130 (top)
Courtesy of Sanderson/www.sanderson-us.com, 12; 18; 37; 82; 117; 122; 123
Courtesy of Shabby Chic/www.shabbychic.com, 84
Courtesy of Spiegel/www.spiegel.com, 114 (top)
Tim Street-Porter/www.beateworks.com, 52; 102
Courtesy of Tile Source, 38
Brian Vanden Brink, 108 (top); 127
Brian Vanden Brink/Joe Dixon Architect/Christine Maclin Interior Design, 107
Brian Vanden Brink/Antonia Munroe, Artist, 25
Victoria & Albert Museum, London, Great Britain/Art Resource, NY, 54 (middle); 133
Andreas von Einsiedel, 26 (left); 58 (top); 62 (top); 73; 75; 77; 88; 114 (bottom); 118 (left); 121 (top left)
Andreas von Einsiedel/Elizabeth Whiting & Associates, 23
Dominique Vorillon, 46
Courtesy of J.P. Weaver, 101
Alan Weintraub, 54 (bottom)
Jennifer Wills, 142
Jennifer Wills/Meera Lester, Artist, 19
Courtesy of Zimmer + Rohde/www.zimmer-rohde.com, Ardecora, Etamine and Zimmer + Rohde, 2; 3; 5; 6; 10; 13; 16; 17

About the Authors

Meera Lester is an internationally published writer based in San Jose, California. Her most recent book, written with Marsha Janda-Rosenberg, is *Adventures in Mosaics: Creating Pique Assiette Mosaics from Broken China, Glass, Pottery, and Found Treasures.* An oil painter and avid gardener, she loves growing beautiful flowers to paint and to use in decorating her home.

A. Bronwyn Llewellyn is a veteran writer, scholar, and exhibit developer whose prestigious credits include the Smithsonian, the National Civil Rights Museum, the Harry S. Truman Library, the Oregon Historical Museum, and The Tech Museum of Innovation. She holds a bachelor's degree in English from William Jewell College and a master's degree in museum studies from the Cooperstown Graduate Program in New York. She is the author of *Goddess at Home: Divine Interiors Inspired by Aphrodite, Artemis, Athena, Demeter, Hera, Hestia, and Persephone* and *The Shakespeare Oracle.* She lives in the San Francisco Bay area.

Acknowledgments

I extend a huge thank-you to my co-writer, A. Bronwyn Llewellyn, whose exceptional skills at researching and writing shine through this work; to Jan Stiles, whose exuberant and skillful copyedits rendered a more readable manuscript; to Leeanna Franklin, whose ideas about authentic country interiors inspired a section of this book; and to the team at Rockport Publishers, whose collective vision enabled us to bring the germinal seed of this idea to its glorious blooming fruition.

Meera Lester

Once again the talented team at Rockport has melded words and pictures into a beautiful book. Editor Mary Ann Hall makes the process seem easy. Photo editor Betsy Gammons always finds just the right image for just the right spot. Jan Stiles's copyedits caught the errors and smoothed the prose. Bouquets of gratitude to them as well as to publisher Winnie Prentiss, art director Silke Braun, senior designer Regina Grenier, managing editor Kristy Mulkern, and image librarian Cora Hawks. And last, but certainly not least, my deepest appreciation goes to Meera Lester, who is a joy to work with and a wonderful friend.

A. Bronwyn Llewellyn